THE BOMB HEARD AROUND THE WORLD

THE LIVES AND DEATHS OF HARRY T. & HARRIETTE V. MOORE

Top Cat II Production Publishing Group, LLC
244 Fifth Avenue, Suite 2555
New York, New York, 10001

The Bomb Heard Around The World
The Lives and Deaths of Harry T. & Harriette V. Moore

Top Cat II Production Publishing Group®
are registered trademarks of Top Cat II Production Publishing Group (USA)

First Edition: May, 2019

ISBN-10: 0-692-92587-2
ISBN-13: 978-0-692-92587-4

Cover Design by Lauren Garza of Two Easily Amused
Book layout by Gail Kaiser
Library of Congress Control Number: 2017950763
Printed in the United States of America
10 9 8 7 6 5 4 3 2 1

THE BOMB HEARD AROUND THE WORLD
THE LIVES AND DEATHS OF HARRY T. & HARRIETTE V. MOORE

"A man may die, nations may rise and fall, but an idea lives on".
~ *President John F. Kennedy*
Where there is no vision, the people perish:
~ *Proverbs 29:18 (KJV)*

GREGORY MARQUETTE

DEDICATED TO THE MEMORIES OF HARRY, HARRIETTE,
JUANITA EVANGELINE & ANNIE ROSALEA MOORE

"What lies behind us
and what lies before us
are tiny matters compared to what lies within us."

⁓ Ralph Waldo Emerson

"In Honor of those that carried the first candle to light the way"

⁓ DRS

"Harry and Harriette Moore are important figures in the civil rights movement. Shining a light on their story, bringing closure to their untimely, horrific deaths, will keep their work and legacy alive for generations to come.

The words and example set by the Moore Family are more important now than ever. We need more people willing to stand in the gap of inequality to fight for what's right. Their life's work is an inspiration to us all."

United States Congressman Charlie Crist
Florida's 13th District

"There's a positive result just by knowing
that somebody cares and that these things
will not be left to stand, that there is a
rightness about what is being done."

"Whenever you're trying to pursue the truth
or trying to pursue justice, that's a good
thing. We should never become a
society that's stops doing that."

~ *Congressman Charlie Crist*

Harry and Harriette Moore

There are many reasons to write if one has the will and the patience, but this book offered much more in the writing, once facts revealed themselves. What I learned in this process was alarming, yet inspiring; terrifying, yet brilliant; honorable, yet evil, and most definitely brutal.

When you set out to study a subject, tell a story, offer a point of view, very often surprises come tumbling your way. One thing is sure: every writer's journey provides twists and turns that could never have been predicted nor imagined. To say this journey delivered would be an understatement.

I first came across the names of Harry and Harriette Moore during the writing of a screenplay about a group of young black painters in Florida called "The Highwaymen" who had first gained notoriety in the late 1950's into the 60's. Their stories are remarkable. However, during the research process, I learned of a schoolteacher named Harry Tyson Moore. They called him "Professor Moore."

His story was astonishing; it affected me profoundly. In my view, there was no question. Instantly, I knew that his accounting had to be told; a light must shine brightly on the Moore family for reasons which are profoundly consequential to all of us. Much has been written about Harry T. Moore in Florida, but on a national level, his life had not been presented or celebrated in a manner befitting his contributions to America.

His life and achievements are of significant historical importance. The risks and sacrifices made by Harry and Harriette Moore and their children benefit America in a way for which we should all be immensely grateful.

While the story of Harry T. Moore is about history, it should also be considered a cautionary tale where, if we are not careful, history may easily become prologue. Moreover, this history is one we dare not repeat. America must not let his fate be a prologue to more injustice. We should not allow today's prejudices and race crimes to be a preview for more racial abuses to come, in the name of ignorance, fear, and hatred.

However, sadly, history has proven that human beings do tend to repeat mistakes, and with the current political climate, it is evident that there are pockets of society which have devolved to the extent that 'Jim Crow' behavior has resurfaced prominently in American society.

Today, around the globe, extreme right-wing organizations show themselves without restraint. They are encouraged to reveal themselves with a sense of flawed pride and eager defiance.

But dark chapters in history should be our lessons, not our fates.

History is an infinite overlapping series of causes and effects. It was not long after the deaths of Harry and Harriette Moore that civil rights could no longer be ignored or taken for granted with so many courageous African Americans stepping forward to risk their lives, too.

In 1951, the court of public opinion generated enormous international condemnation of the cowardly acts perpetrated on the Moore family. Many foreign governments expressed their joint indignation and disappointment in America. People around the globe were outraged that this country, which touted liberty, freedom, equality, democracy, and opportunity, could allow such dreadful racist behavior.

Soon civil rights would take a prominent position in the American consciousness with the brave actions of Rosa Parks, Medgar Evers, Malcolm X, Martin Luther King and many, many more.

Harry and Harriette Moore opened the door...

PREFACE

This book is not a comprehensive presentation of Harry T. Moore's life nor is it an in-depth look at the history of race relations in Florida.

There are historical events, complexities, politics, and investigations spread over many decades which would have to be analyzed and cross-referenced over several volumes to suffice, were this the goal. This book is written, instead, with a different purpose. With African American history and civil rights education lacking in American education, the intention of this writing is to shed light on historical events which are fundamental turning points in the development of race relations in America.

By focusing on Harry T. Moore, we gain a 'birds-eye' view of a society in upheaval during one of the most transformative decades in American history. He was a precursor, a trigger, of sorts, who instigated crucial changes in the lives of African Americans in their quest for legitimate civil rights.

I hope to make readers aware of many essential dynamics which were tipping points for change, by discussing Harry Tyson Moore and his family. He made an enormous impact on America, yet his contributions, for the most part, have been ignored. The Moore family paid the ultimate price for their actions and, hopefully, this book will shed light on their remarkable story.

While some may know of him in Florida, on a national level, Harry T. Moore has not been given the attention, respect, and appreciation he and his family deserve for their enormous contributions to this nation. He emerged at the beginning of a crucially important chapter in America's history, and events surrounding his life set the stage for a turbulent future urgently in need of course correction.

Thankfully, many decades later, there are dedicated individuals and civic-minded organizations still working hard to chronicle these critical events and preserve the memory of this family which sacrificed so much for their belief in 'actual' freedom and justice in America; by 'actual' I mean living day-to-day freedom, as opposed to freedom 'on paper' only.

It is now time for a national audience to be aware of the remarkable work and courageous efforts of Harry T. Moore. In today's polarized, volatile socio-political climate, memories of decades gone by echo eerily from afar. Mr. Moore's life is a cautionary chapter from which we ought to learn - but it may not be enough.

Jim Crow-like actions have crept back into our daily lives in ways one could never have imagined with such disturbing events as the alt-right, white-supremacist march in Charlottesville, Virginia, and a polarized America coming face-to-face with formerly hidden hatreds, now 'out of the closet', operating with the courage of ignorance.

The killings of Michael Brown in Ferguson, Missouri and Trayvon Martin in Sanford, Florida are only the tip of an ever-growing iceberg of hideous racial violence signifying a systemic, racially-prejudiced stain, weakening American society and tarnishing its image around the world.

The much overused statement: 'we must not forget history for fear of repeating it', is appropriate here. However, I take issue with this statement. In my view, just 'not forgetting history' is not enough.

Remembering and then participating in a solution is better.

~ *Gregory Marquette*

CONTENTS

CONTENTS

"Freedom never descends upon a people.
It is always bought with a price."

∼ Harry T. Moore

Chapter 1

HARRY T. MOORE

AFTER WORLD WAR II

Histori is where we come from. Now is the opportunity to disallow history from becoming our prologue. By 1945, the global impact of World War ll had forever changed the course of history.

With so many countries uniting to halt the Nazi regime, its conclusion sent cautionary shock waves around the planet as to what can happen when liberty and freedom are savagely threatened. The end of that war and the return from overseas of so many young men and women signaled to America that the nation was ready for a change.

World War 1, the Great Depression, and World War ll were unparalleled catastrophes; they shook America to its core. War-torn foreign countries experienced, first hand, what that fight for freedom cost and now many young black Americans could see clearly, upon their arrival back home, that what they had fought for in foreign lands was not available to them in their own country.

The divide between whites and blacks in America has a history which pre-dates the formation of the country.

Throughout history, the DNA of this country has been infected with attitudes, beliefs, actions, fear, and violence which has impacted American society profoundly, and still does today.

The Civil War, Reconstruction, and many Supreme Court Decisions set America on a dark path, riddled with complexities, misunderstandings, anger, terror, and racism. This land of liberty, equality, opportunity, and freedom was anything but, for people of color, of different faiths, and different nationalities.

In America's South, these brutal realities were magnified exponentially for Americans of color.

MIMS, FLORIDA

Harry Tyson Moore and his wife, Harriette, with their two daughters, Evangeline and Annie, lived in Mims, Florida.

Mims was a small town (and still is) located at the north end of Brevard County, north of Titusville. And Titusville is approximately seventeen miles from Cape Canaveral Air Force Station, which was the facility the United States Government used in 1949 for rocket and missile testing.

The town of Mims was named after a man named Casper Mims who arrived in the area in 1876 to open its first grocery store. The town grew rapidly once the railroad arrived in 1885 and Mims soon became a citrus center when businessman Thomas Nevins developed citrus groves and called his enterprise the Nevins Fruit Company.

It is located two hundred and fifty miles north of Miami, in Brevard County which is the heart of citrus country (as it's called). Situated on the banks of Indian River, Mims is separated by a long ribbon of land near the ocean.

The fact is, you could drive through Mims and possibly not even know it, back in the 1940's or 50's. Its presence was well-disguised by the abundance of orange groves.

In other words, it was a 'backwoods' Florida town with only a few streets consisting of pleasant-looking homes in which the citrus owners resided.

However, on the outskirts of this town, just off Highway 1, is where you could find the 'backbone' of the town and its industry. There you could see only shabby, unpainted clapboard bungalows, often described as 'shotgun' homes, filled with hundreds of destitute African Americans scratching out a meager living.

Mims was, for many years, a place where people usually passed through on the way to someplace bigger - or at least more inviting.

CHRISTMAS DAY

On Christmas Day in 1951, there was a thick fog hanging over Mims. During winter months Mims often saw fog, so it was not unusual, particularly in this region of Florida. People who lived there usually installed fog lights on their vehicles to adjust to these typical winter weather patterns.

At Mims' outskirts, in these orange groves, sat a tiny 'shotgun' house which was the home of Harry T. Moore and his family.

'Shotgun' was the proper name for this type of home; they were common in Mims. It meant that the back door and front door aligned directly. These types of houses were always small, rectangular, narrow, and raised up on cinder blocks. Homes like these were generally an indication of poverty.

On Christmas Day evening a sedan pulled over to park on a patch of dirt outside the home of Harry T. Moore. In the car were his wife, Harriette, his mother Rosa, and one of his two daughters, named Annie. His second daughter, Evangeline, was on her way home by train from her job in Washington, D.C., to join the Christmas festivities.

Exiting the car was Harry T. Moore; otherwise known as "Professor Moore" by most people, with the rest to follow.

In the late afternoon, the Moore Family had Christmas dinner at his mother-in-law's house, nearby. They had returned home to complete their Christmas evening and turn in for the night. Harry had also planned a private moment to celebrate a 25th wedding anniversary salute to his wife, Harriette.

The Moore house exterior looked much the same as those belonging to adjacent Mims citrus workers, but the inside was pure Harry and Harriette. They were both dedicated to education and its importance registered on the bookshelves. They were chockfull of history, sociology, poetry, and English literature.

Harriette had her upright piano, and Harry's radio sat on a table beside the sofa so he could hear his newscasts, and on Sunday mornings he'd listen to the Mormon Tabernacle Choir. There was a Victrola record player in the living room, ready to spin any of their spiritual, blues or jazz records, sitting neatly on the floor.

Because Harry often worked at home for his NAACP and Voter Registration preparations, he had an old manual typewriter, and a copy device called a Ditto machine in the corner of his dining room. A Ditto copier was also called "a spirit duplicator" (because it used spirits (alcohol) to make copies). As well, Ditto machines didn't need electricity; perfect for Harry's extra-curricular political activities.

Harriette announced that she was tired, but Harry wouldn't hear of it. He wanted to share a piece of holiday cake with his wife to commemorate their wedding anniversary. They sat together and shared special memories of their two and a half decades together. Harry offered a short speech to his wife to memorialize the particular moment. They finished their cake, plates were cleared, and Harriette headed off to bed.

Annie (whom they called 'Peaches'), laid down on the sofa to read for a short time; but soon she left for her bedroom, too.

Harry and his mother, Rosa, sat together to talk. She re-expressed her concerns about the dangers of his voter registration and NAACP activities. Rosa was aware of the many threats made against her son. "Every advancement comes by way of sacrifice," he always responded. "What I am doing is for the benefit of my race." Harry would not be swayed to curtail what he believed to be his mission.

It was just past ten o'clock. Harry and Rosa said goodnight, and she made her way to the guest room at the back of the house. Harry turned off the lights and moved to his bedroom.

Outside, the winter fog had engulfed the orange grove as it typically did this time of year. It was a quiet Florida winter's holiday night.

10:20 P.M.

A thunderous explosion suddenly lifted the Moore house up and off its cinder block foundation. The detonation erupted directly beneath the floor joists under Harry and Harriette's bed. The bedroom was instantly shredded. Jagged pieces of the roof collapsed into the bedroom as its walls blew apart in jigsaw-shaped pieces which became flying projectiles hurtling across the terrain outside.

The bone-chilling thump of the detonation was heard up to four miles away in Titusville. The concussion awakened sleeping neighbors who lived within

Home of Harry T. and Harriette V. Moore after a bomb exploded, 1951
(photo courtesy of State Archives of Florida, Florida Memory, http://floridamemory.com/items/show/4512)

Harry & Harriette Moore

a few miles, in all directions. Stunned residents bolted from their homes, fearing some further calamity may strike again at any moment.

The massive bomb placed under Harry and Harriette Moore's bedroom was precisely positioned to explode under their bed; the most effective choice for a location to be sure the prime 'targets' were taken out.

Whoever built the explosive device must have been a professional or an experienced amateur.

Pieces of the Moore home lie strewn across the landscape. Tattered Christmas cards, torn voter registration guidelines, and crumpled pieces of NAACP pamphlets lie muddied underfoot while debris and jagged chunks of the Moore's bedroom lie scattered in a semi-circle around the shattered home.

Throughout the night, a somber collection of on-lookers gathered to study the devastation, weep for their friends, and discuss which perpetrators could have committed such a savage crime. As the sun rose, more neighbors, friends, citrus workers, teachers, students, families, with police officers, arrived at the bomb site and stayed well into the afternoon.

It seemed, however, that not all the visitors were friendly. Many white visitors, (other than law enforcement), also arrived to have a look. Allegedly some were not so sad.

Estimates suggest over one thousand visitors had arrived at the Moore bomb site by late afternoon.

The only hospital in the area was in Sanford, a small town, over an hour away from Mims (driving in 1951). Harry's brother-in-law, George Simms, frantically drove Harry, bleeding, and moaning, in the back seat of his car. Harry died before arriving at the hospital. A car today could have gotten there sooner, but it would not likely have made a difference. Harry's injuries were too severe.

At the time of the Moore bombing an oxygen-equipped ambulance may have been available at the E.A. Smith Funeral Home in Titusville, 4 1/2 miles away from Mims. It is not known if any contact was made with this funeral home to acquire the use of the ambulance to transport the Moores to the hospital; however, the racial attitudes at that time would most likely have prohibited 'colored' people from being carried in a white ambulance.

Harriette Moore did make it to the hospital and lived long enough to visit her murdered husband at the mortuary, to say goodbye.

Harriette V. Moore

Upon her return to the hospital, she said her goodbyes to her two daughters.

They begged her to fight for her life, but according to sources, she had given up. She stated that, with Harry gone, she had nothing left to live for. Soon a blood clot formed in her lung. Harriette Moore passed away nine days after the bombing on January 4th, 1952.

WIFE OF VICTIM OF
CHRISTMAS BOMBING DIES

New York Herald Tribune, Friday, January 4, 1952
By The United Press

Left Hospital Tuesday for Husband's Funeral;
F.B.I. Continues Florida Probe

Sanford, FL, Jan. 3 Mrs. Harriet Moore, forty-nine, wife of Harry T. Moore, bomb slaying victim, died in a hospital here today of injuries received in the Christmas night bombing of the Negro leader's home at Mims, FL.

Dr. George H. Starke said death was caused by a blood clot. Mrs. Moore had been improving steadily until Tuesday, the day of her husband's funeral. She left the hospital that day against Dr. Starke's orders to view Mr. Moore's body at a funeral home. Mr. Moore, forty-six, was Florida secretary of the National Association for the Advancement of Colored People. Both he and his wife were school teachers.

Brevard County authorities and the Federal Bureau of Investigation have been investigating the bombing but have made no report.

At the time of Mr. Moore's funeral Tuesday, F.B.I. Agents completed a piece-by-piece examination of the rubble of the bombed home. At an earlier inquest, County Judge V. B. Carlton said the bomb had been placed directly under Mr. Moore's bed. Officials so far have not said what type of explosive was used.

One of the Moore's two daughters, Annie (Peaches), was also in the small frame home in another bedroom when the explosion took place. She was not injured. The second daughter, Evangeline, had not arrived for the family reunion Christmas night.

Assistant State Attorney Hubert E. Griggs and J. J. Elliott, special investigator for Governor Fuller Warren tried to get a statement about the bombing from Mrs. Moore yesterday.

THE FUNERAL

The St. James Missionary Baptist Church was the location for Harry T. Moore's funeral. It was a traumatic event for the community and blacks, in general, in Florida and America. There was no actual count of the guests at the funeral, but the unofficial attendance estimate was reported as high as one thousand people.

Because of the brutal circumstances of his death, guards were posted outside the church during the service, in case another attack occurred. There was a good reason to believe it might. Tensions ran high. Not one newspaper implicated the Klan or a possibility thereof. No arrests were made. The NAACP announced that Mr. Moore's last rites would be held New Year's Day at Mims in St. James Missionary Baptist Church, a mile from his demolished home.

The service was scheduled to be approximately one hour long, but with so many guests in attendance and so many guest speakers, it went considerably longer. It seemed all eyes in America were on Harry T. Moore's death. He had become famous in his death and a symbol for the times in which they lived.

Many additional mourners from Miami had planned to attend the funeral. A sizable group of white and black representatives from Miami organizations had intended to drive to Mims to stand with black mourners. However, false bulletins were posted in newspapers indicating the funeral was delayed. This was, of course, untrue. It was rumored that Ku Klux Klan members or those sympathetic, posted false announcements to prevent people from attending.

The funeral procession to the LaGrange Cemetery was over a mile long. Ironically, Harry was buried in a segregated cemetery. The absurdities and injustices of the time continued.

Presiding over the funeral, Reverend J.W. Bruno recited a final hymn for Harry T. Moore as they lowered him into the ground.

He uttered one final thought aloud: "You can kill the prophet, but you cannot kill the message."

Viewing remains of Harry T. Moore, Negroes from all over Florida attended funeral. Moore's wife was in hospital at time of funeral. Moore was a Methodist but service was held at the Baptist church, only one big enough to hold crowd.

Standing behind Moore's open coffin, assistant state attorney Hubert E. Griggs addresses funeral crowd. Griggs aided in investigation, claimed he could not conceive that Moore's death was caused by any citizen of Brevard County, the location of the Moore farm.

Signing register in church, hundreds pause to pay tribute to Moore. Weeping bitterly, family of murdered man sits in sorrow (below) as body is lowered into grave. Moore's wife left hospital to view body, died several days later.

BOMBING CLIMAXED SERIES OF OUTRAGES

RACE VIOLENCE in Florida flared often during the past year but it took the bomb murder of Florida NAACP leader Harry T. Moore to focus worldwide attention on violence in the state.

Racial tension in the state has been building up ever since four Negro youths were arrested in Lake County in 1949 and charged with the rape of a young white housewife. One of the youths was killed by a posse, the three others were tried and one was given life while Samuel Shepherd and Walter Lee Irvin, both 23, were sentenced to death. The NAACP led a fight to free the condemned men and the U. S. Supreme Court reversed the decision. Death entered the picture again when Sheriff Willis V. McCall killed Shepherd and wounded Irvin, claiming they had tried to escape while being taken to Tavares for a court hearing. Known as the "Groveland Case" and "The Little Scottsboro Case," the trials and the "legal murder" stirred up strong feelings both among Negroes and whites.

The Groveland Case was but one incident in a series of violent racial incidents during 1951. Prior to the lynching of Melvin Womack, another Negro, Willie Vincent, had been beaten by three white men and tossed from a speeding car with a fractured skull. In the same area, Luther Coleman, a Negro janitor at the Winter Garden elementary school, was beaten up by white men and a teen-age shoe shine boy, Jimmy Woodards, was shot five times but recovered.

Moore spoke out against the floggings and beatings. He was interested in the Groveland case and campaigned for the prosecution of the sheriff that shot the two Negro youths in the case.

Moore was well thought of by most whites in the area. One business man in nearby Orlando who had known Moore in political work said Moore was a "level-headed man with a deep feeling for his people. Moore wasn't an extremist. He wasn't a rabble-rouser."

Quiet and controlled as they were, Moore's speeches and his activities were enough to enflame many Southern whites against him. When he and his wife retired on Christmas night after a ham and turkey dinner with his mother, his daughter Annie, and his wife's brother, M/Sgt. George Simms who had just returned from Korea, it was just a little after 10 p.m. The family had not opened their Christmas presents for they were waiting for Moore's daughter Evangeline to come home from Washington, D. C.

Moore never got to see what was in the gaily-wrapped packages. About ten minutes after the lights were turned out in the modest cottage, someone placed a powerful explosive (probably nitroglycerine) under the wooden floor and the blast fatally injured both Moore and his wife.

Ebony • November, 1975

Continued on Page 46

Photo top left: Viewing remains of Harry T. Moore, Negroes from all over Florida attended the funeral. Moore's wife was in the hospital at the time of funeral. Moore was a Methodist but service was held at the Baptist church, the only one big enough to hold the crowd.

Photo center left: Signing register in church, hundreds pause to pay tribute to Moore. Weeping bitterly, family of murdered man sits in sorrow (photo bottom left) as body is lowered into grave. Moore's wife left hospital to view body, died several days later.

Only six weeks earlier, Harry Moore had forcefully called for the indictment of Sheriff Willis McCall, the senior law enforcement officer who shot two of the four black Groveland Four defendants while transporting them in his police car for retrial.

McCall had significant ties to the Ku Klux Klan. No one disputed this, not even McCall himself. During his career in law enforcement, he had earned over fifty 'racial' infractions, assorted lawsuits, indictments, and inquiries over his severely questionable behavior, including incidents where black defendants died in his custody.

Everyone knew about McCall. But no one ever did anything or chose not to; not until the final chapter of his career.

Five months after Harry and Harriette Moore were assassinated, on May 6, 1952, Sheriff Willis McCall was reelected for another term, as sheriff, (his third) by what locals called 'a landslide.'

This was McCall's shining moment and considered a significant triumph after the highly controversial Groveland case.

GARY CORSAIR INTERVIEW

Gary Corsair is the author of *Legal Lynching: The Sad Saga of the Groveland Four*. His book and remarkable research were important in the re-telling of the Groveland Four and Harry T. Moore elements of this book. Mr. Corsair won 15 awards during his newspaper career. He has worked as a reporter, editor, and publisher. In 1992, he had launched newspapers and served as editor of The Zephyr Hills News, Tri-County Sun, and The Villages Daily Sun. He has also worked as a TV reporter, anchor, and news director.

GARY: I came across the Groveland story while I was working as a television reporter. It took eleven years researching, writing, and rewriting my book, The Groveland Four.

GREGORY: Did you feel that the Groveland Four case was a possible tipping point between blacks and whites in Florida? Could this case have been a contributing factor or trigger to motivate the assassinations of Harry and Harriette Moore?

GARY: I think not only that, but I think that the sheriff (in the
Groveland Four case), Willis McCall, was probably, (at least
indirectly), involved in the bombing of the Moore family.
Some witnesses thought they saw him at the Moore's (home)
before the bombing. I think he (McCall)was sending a message
not only to blacks in Groveland but throughout Florida.
I don't think there's any doubt in my mind that Sheriff McCall
indirectly had a hand in it. I don't know that he ordered it
directly, but I think he was smart enough to have a couple
of layers between himself and the guys who put the dynamite
under the Moore's house. It's the kind of brazen act he
would do.

GREGORY: The way blacks are treated today, in the south particularly,
does it feel like America is revisiting pre-Civil War values?

GARY: I think to a large degree, yes. It (racism) persists to this day.

Three weeks later, the NAACP announced that Harry Moore would be
awarded the 1952 Spingarn Medal (posthumously), the NAACP's highest
honor, given to the African American whose achievements were judged to
be most outstanding for that year.

Many felt it was a shame he could not have been given the award while he
was alive.

On July 27th, Harry Moore's mother, Rosa, accepted the Spingarn Medal in
his name. Her words were powerful:

"The crusade for freedom has claimed many martyrs, but none deserves
accolade more than Harry T. Moore who, on Christmas night, 1951, paid
with his life for his devotion to human freedom.....Harry T. Moore, working
in an atmosphere of official interference, and hostility, lived with death...
He refused to be intimidated. He rejected bribes. He turned his back on
cajolery.... He fought consistently and courageously against all the sinister

manifestations of racism which flourished in his home state.... His martyr-dom in the truest exemplifies the truth that "Greater love hath no man than this, that a man lay down his life for his friends."

It was 'a given' that Harry T. Moore had acquired an 'army of enemies' because of his high-profile civil rights activities over the years. Where the Moore assassinations were concerned, the unofficial consensus within the general population was: 'it had to be the Klan,' and further, the consensus favored Willis McCall as its leading culprit.

Harry T. Moore had earned the unique title of being the first NAACP official murdered in the struggle for modern civil rights. He was now, officially, a martyr for his cause.

"No one's life can be encompassed in one telling.
There is no way to give each year its allotted weight,
to include each event, each person
who helped to shape a lifetime.
What can be done is to be faithful in spirit
to the record, and try to find one's way
to the heart of the man."

~ John Richard Briley (Screenwriter, "Gandhi")

December 25th, 1951, at 10:20 p.m.,
a bomb exploded under Harry Moore's house
killing him and his wife.

Chapter 2
THE CRIME

Harry T. Moore was a bold and courageous man, ahead of his time; and dangerously so, in the eyes of the 'white establishment.'

Yet he had no following, no flock, no congregation, no brand, no money, no office, and no power. And he was black. He was not the obvious candidate to stand-up to 'white-dominated' America in the 1940's & 50's. He was a quiet, humble man, and not an excellent orator, but he had intelligence, integrity, elegance, and self-respect.

And he was fearless.

He entered the political activism fray early in his life; beginning his quest in the 1930's.

He was the real thing: a genuine civil rights activist long before 'civil rights activism' had a label, was acknowledged, or even dared to exist. But it was not a label he was seeking or even acknowledgement for his efforts. He was just tired of the indignities, the humiliations, the injustices. It was the actions that mattered. And he would be relentless.

WILLIAM GARY INTERVIEW

William Gary's professional background is engineering. He graduated from a segregated high school, then attended Tennessee State University in Nashville, Tennessee. He majored in electrical engineering and entered a work-study program which eventually led him to work at the Kennedy Space Center. Upon graduation, he joined NASA to work at the Design Engineering Directorate for eighteen years. After that, he moved to Payloads Directorate, where he joined a team to process satellites. He has since retired after forty years of government service.

GREGORY: Why are Harry and Harriette Moore not recognized for their work? They were extraordinarily active in civil rights, well before Brown vs. The Board of Education Supreme Court decision in 1954.

BILL: And that's why you won't find the Moores in most history books. They came before Brown vs. The Board of Education, which, in most peoples' minds was the starting point for modern civil rights. Add to that the fact that Harry and Harriette Moore lived in a remote area of Florida dating back to the 1930's and 40's when there was no internet or television. And the Moores were localized, while communities in the other areas may have had their own activists. In Mississippi, they had Medgar Evers, Alabama had Martin Luther King Jr., and so forth.

GREGORY: So who would know about Harry T. Moore?

BILL: Only historians and academics and people in Mims who had relatives alive to tell the story. The average person, unless they studied history, would likely not be aware of Harry T. Moore.

GREGORY: And their deaths were a first in several important respects?

BILL: That's true. We refer to Harry and Harriette Moore as the first martyrs of the modern Civil Rights movement. They were the first official NAACP leaders to be killed while carrying out the work of the NAACP. There have been other people assassinated but you won't find a couple that was killed purely because of their involvement with the NAACP (and other actions associated with their activities.).

GREGORY: But in other states, there were black activists?

BILL: It's true. But Harry T. Moore was the first Executive Secretary of a state conference. That is when you bring all these different branches together and form them into one organization. He was the first one to do that. Of course, now every state has a state conference. Alabama, Georgia, Texas, Pennsylvania, New York. All of them have state conferences. There are branches throughout the nation plus in five or six foreign countries.

GREGORY: But here in the state of Florida, at that time, Harry went out on his own and created new branches?

BILL: He did - and he was the first to organize all those branches into a state-wide organization. So regarding martyrs, he was the first, a long time before Malcolm X and Martin Luther King.

~

Harry Moore saw so much in America that offended him. This was his America. The land of freedom and liberty - yet the advertising slogan did not match with the reality. It was not the country he had envisioned for his children and race. In his view, it had to change, and he was going to help it along - no matter what.

A SPECIAL APPEAL TO THE RELIGIOUS, FRATERNAL AND CIVIC LEADERS OF FLORIDA

Mims, Florida
October 14, 1947

Dear Co-Workers:

We have been working earnestly during the past few months, trying to help spread the spirit of the NAACP over the state of Florida. One year ago there were 61 branches of the NAACP in our state. Today Florida has 78 branches of this great organization scattered from Key West to Pensacola. Our success in this work has been due largely to the splendid co-operation that some of you have given, and for this we wish to express our appreciation.

Whenever we go into a community in an effort to arouse interest in the NAACP, we always seek your support. We usually go to the ministers first; because they are the recognized leaders of our people, and we feel that their blessing should be on any movement that tends to advance the cause of colored people. We hold most of our meetings in churches, because we fully realize that the NAACP is rendering a Christian service to our people.

Two thousand years ago Christ went from place to place on this earth, relieving human suffering and teaching a doctrine of love and fair play. Today the NAACP is doing a similar work. Just think of the many helpless, innocent Negroes whose lives have been saved by the legal machinery of the NAACP. Just think how many innocent Negroes have been saved from long prison terms through our fight to secure justice in the courts. Do you remember the four Pompano boys who were saved from the electric chair a few years ago? Do you remember Simon Peter Taylor of Tampa?

Do you remember how the Orlando Branch saved the lives of a Negro couple who had to kill a white man in self-defense back in 1943? Do you remember the Columbia, Tennessee, cases? And just three weeks ago the War Department reported that efforts of the NAACP Legal Staff had saved another condemned Negro soldier from being hanged.

Thus for 38 years the NAACP has preached a gospel of justice and equal opportunities for all mankind, without regard to race, creed, or color. This is just a practical application of the Golden Rule proclaimed by Christ: "As ye would that men should do to you, do ye even so to them".

This year the NAACP is trying to register a million members to help support its noble work. Florida's goal for 1947 is 25,000 members. Therefore, we need to get nearly 19,000 members by December 31 in order to reach our quota for this year. We earnestly solicit your support in our fall membership drive. Please urge the members of your organization to join the NAACP.

We wish to designate November as a special "NAACP Month" in Florida. We ask every minister to take a little time at each service during November to tell his congregation about the good work of the NAACP. We also ask each pastor to appoint a worker in his church to collect NAACP memberships during November. These may be turned over to the local branches. (If there is not a branch in your community, please send your memberships to the executive secretary in Mims). We ask the heads of our religious, fraternal and civic organizations to send special messages to your subordinate units, urging their support of the NAACP membership drive. If you will give us space on program during your conferences, associations, conventions, etc., we shall be glad to send representatives to speak to the people.

It is so easy to become a member of the NAACP. You may join for the small fee of $1.00. However, many people are so anxious to help carry the work on that they take out memberships for $2.00, $2.50, $5.00, $10.00, $25.00, and even $500.00. It might be interesting to note that Dr. D. Y. Jamison, president of the National Baptist Convention, recently took out a $500.00 Life Membership in the NAACP. Young people under 21 years of age may take out Youth Memberships for $ .50 per year. There is a type of membership to fit everybody's pocketbook.

We cannot afford to let Florida fall behind other southern states in this effort. Therefore, let us sacrifice a little time and energy. Let us put our combined strength behind this drive to secure Florida's quota for the support of the organization that is fighting so hard to secure a fuller measure of justice for our race.

Sincerely yours,
Harry T. Moore

Harry T. Moore, Executive Secretary
Florida State Conference, NAACP

Early on, Harry became the Executive Secretary of the National Association for the Advancement of Colored People (NAACP) in 1934, when he started a branch in Brevard County. He ran the Florida chapter of the organization, and he was solely responsible for expanding its many chapters across the state. And because the NAACP was not really a political organization, per se, he soon formed the Progressive Voters' League, which he co-founded in 1944, so he could focus on voter registration.

Harry T. Moore was hopeful that his efforts would remedy at least some of the major issues of his era. He was primarily dedicated to the concept of increasing black participation in the voting process.

Voting was a legitimate instrument of change, and he worked tirelessly to make this avenue available for African Americans. Black voters could build this powerful tool to trigger change and then maybe this could finally provide some ammunition against overwhelming injustices perpetrated on blacks in America.

And as a working schoolteacher and principal, he was acutely aware that education was of paramount importance for black children. So Florida needed black teachers to provide this education. This was the only way black children could break out of the historically vicious cycle created by extreme poverty and racism.

However, black teachers' salaries were so far below those of white teachers; so much so that black teachers could barely survive at the grim, deficient income levels imposed by the current education system.

ELOUISE BOATWRIGHT INTERVIEW

Elouise is a resident in Mims. When she was of school age, she attended with Evangeline Moore. She spent time with the Moore family at their home and knew them quite well.

GREGORY: When you were a teenager did Professor Moore talk to you about voting?

ELOUISE: We lived by a church, the church that I go to, and he would have meetings there about voting all the time.

GREGORY: What would he teach you about it?

ELOUISE: How to apply. Civil rights. The voting rules. He was trying to get us, you know, get started voting. The whole Moore family went to the Methodist church right here in Mims, not too far from where I lived.

GREGORY: Do you know how he started on this path - teaching people how to vote?

ELOUISE: In 1934, Professor Moore received a letter from the National Association for the Advancement of Colored People. He said, "This (NAACP) is what I've been looking for." He experienced firsthand the Jim Crow education system in Florida, the hand-me-down books and ramshackle schools where black teachers were routinely paid far less than white teachers. Within a year, Professor Moore founded the Brevard County branch of the NAACP and began to gather evidence to prove that black teachers were being discriminated against. And he spoke at church regularly to talk to the community.

GREGORY: He was serious about getting better wages for black teacher and about voting. Was that brave of him to stand up for these things?

ELOUISE: He was brave. But everybody was afraid for him.

GREGORY: Why were they afraid?

ELOUISE: Because they thought somebody was eventually going to kill him.

~

Going back to 1938 Harry T. Moore, side-by-side with the NAACP, backed a schoolteacher who filed the first-ever lawsuit against the School Board. Gilbert vs. The Board of Public Instruction of Brevard County, Florida was the name on the court filing. But because Gilbert filed a lawsuit, the School Board simply fired him.

Fear and retaliation were always the immediate responses to any form of opposition.

Unfortunately, the higher court (Florida Supreme Court) declined to review the Gilbert case once he was fired from his teaching position. It all seemed hopeless.

But Harry never stopped. Being relentless was a personality trait which seemed to dominate his character. Others would just call him a trouble-maker, stubborn, uppity. It didn't matter what anyone said. Harry's goal was clear. Provide pay raises for black teachers by championing pay parity between blacks and whites. He thought there ought to be fair opportunity and economic stability in an education system still ruled by the 'separate but equal' edict of Jim Crow America.

If he could instigate continuous legal and civil actions against the powers that be; keep up the intense pressure, something good might happen. He wasn't wrong.

Harry began to muster political support on a scale like never before. His efforts (with able assistance from his wife, Harriette, and their two daughters) significantly raised black voter registration in Florida from 16.9% to approximately 31.7%. Estimates exceeded one hundred thousand new black voters.

He continued to toil relentlessly to halt brutal race crimes perpetrated against blacks which, of course, were many. He raised public awareness of police brutality, lynchings, and judiciary misconduct in hopes of bringing some semblance of justice for the many African American victims and their families.

It would be many years after his passing that the process he initiated would gain sufficient momentum to make a significant difference. But this process had to start somewhere. It was the Brown vs. The Board of Education Supreme Court decision in 1954 when a 'tipping point' would make its mark. Black voices would eventually begin to be heard.

Harry T. Moore was so early in his civil rights efforts, trailblazing his way across a state dominated by "white rule" trying to build a "black base." He had a vision of what could be and what should be. And it was for these reasons that his life had been threatened many times. He knew he was a target.

Law enforcement knew it. His friends knew. His co-workers knew. His family knew. Not that it would do much good - but Harry bought a handgun - just in case.

He continued to write urgent letters to government agencies and law enforcement to challenge racial injustices, police brutality, and race crimes. He wrote stern letters to governors, lawyers, city officials, judges, police departments, government administrators, member of Congress, and senators. He was unafraid to confront anyone, no matter what their station. He was fearless; some would say to a fault. He wanted to make sure his voice was heard, and it was.

The system in America was 'rigged' against African Americans. While many whites and blacks supported his efforts and respected him greatly, there were as many who did not want to listen or even be seen with him, for fear of the effect his 'rocking the boat' might have. Reprisal and retaliation against blacks who were 'too vocal' (or 'too uppity') were standing responses from white supremacists and their kind.

Punishments against blacks were delivered in the form of violence, loss of employment, property damage, death threats, kidnapping, torture, and more.

None of this deterred Harry T. Moore. It did not faze him, or so it seemed. He stated many times that this mission for his people was his duty, no matter what it took, no matter what it cost.

His political activities occurred many years before the actions of the nationally known heroes and martyrs who we have come to regard as 'game changers' in the pursuit of civil rights for African Americans.

Harry T. Moore's actions would be followed and amplified many years later by some of the most important and prominent political figures across the nation, for which many would receive medals, public recognition, media coverage, honors, accolades, holidays named after them, even postage stamps, to salute their deeds.

The fact is: being the first is hard. And Harry was alone.

Harry T. Moore was viewed by many Southern whites, (and some blacks who did not want him to make waves), as 'a troublemaker.' But in Harry's view, a status quo which yielded apathy, injustice, murder, mayhem, savage racism, and racially-motivated hate crimes against African Americans was not to be tolerated.

He knew that voting was a powerful tool to affect change and most blacks had not been allowed to vote or were not aware of its potential, or they had abandoned the idea because of threats, fear, and intimidation by whites who wanted to abolish or at least minimize black voting.

But after many years of hard work his efforts began to show results in the black community. He became a political force registering thousands of new black voters in Florida.

"For nearly two decades he moved silently across the state - through small towns where no restaurant would serve him, no motel would house him, and some gas stations wouldn't let him fill his gas tank, use the bathroom or the telephone.' He traveled from town to town educating black Floridians, in hopes of helping them to register. "

JUANITA BARTON INTERVIEW

Juanita is the youngest of seven children. Some of her brothers and sisters were close friends with the Moore Family. She went to the same schools at Evangeline and Annie (Peaches). Most of her career was spent working for the Martin Marietta company. She spent twenty-two years there before going to Brevard Community College, (now called Florida Eastern). Finally she took a position at the Harry T. and Harriette V. Moore Cultural Center and Museum.

GREGORY: Did Harry and Harriette make a difference?

JUANITA: Absolutely. Harry started the NAACP, but then when he realized that the NAACP had nothing to do with the voting and he felt that voting was more important than civic engagement. He started The Progressive Voters' League and began registering people to vote in this area. Churches at that time were very involved with communities and he would go to different churches to get people registered. Most people were not well-educated or knowledgeable about politics, what it meant, and how it affected them. He would do the research and come up with a ballot. Then people would always know how to vote. Mims had block voting so whoever he supported, everybody supported that person.

GREGORY: Can you please define "block voting"?

JUANITA: 'Block voting' is simply where everyone is voting for the same purpose. There were not enough blacks voting in order to win an election. However, we could affect the outcome of an election. Because everybody voting for the same person gives them a leg up. So they depended on Harry for that. And block voting lasted for a long time after they (Harry and Harriette) were bombed. My parents would still go to the church (to learn who to vote for) because there was someone else who'd taken over after Harry. The block voting itself stayed in place. They would come home from church with their ballot and that's exactly how they would vote.

GREGORY: You attribute that methodology to Harry and Harriet Moore?

JUANITA: Exactly.

GREGORY: Later on Harry and Harriette were both fired for seeking wage parity for black teachers?

JUANITA: True. And we found where my dad signed off on a paper to the School Board that was challenging their firing. That was probably not a good thing because my dad had seven children, and he couldn't afford to lose his job. My daddy was a migrant worker.

GREGORY: Who was responsible for the Moore's termination?

JUANITA: It was the school board. They said Harry was an agitator.

Harry investigated murders, lynchings and a multitude of race crimes committed in his state. He wrote, boldly and regularly, to confront state officials, the courts, and law enforcement officers, to protest the injustices inflicted daily on African Americans.

Harry was not timid to challenge the infamous 'Jim Crow' methods employed by the State of Florida. To press his point he wrote to all levels of government and law enforcement, including the Florida Delegation of the United States Congress.

LETTER TO FLORIDA DELEGATION AT THE UNITED STATES CONGRESS

Mims, Florida
June 13,1947

Florida Delegation
United States Congress
Washington, D. C.

Dear Sirs:

Again we must remind you of the urgent need of a strong Federal law against lynching and mob violence. The recent acquittal of self-confessed lynchers in Greenville, S.C., affords additional proof that the individual states are unable to cope with this great evil.

And our own state is no exception. No doubt you still remember the several lynchings that have blotted Florida's record during the past few months: (1) ....Colles Harrison at Marianna in 1943, (2) Willie James Howard near Live Oak in 1944, (3) ....Jesse James Payne near Madison in 1945, and (4) Sam McFadden at Branford in 1945. These are the recorded lynchings. There have been rumors and strong evidence of others. For example, on January 7, 1946, Leroy Bradwell, a Negro veteran of Midway, Fla., mysteriously disappeared while in the custody of Sheriff Edwards and Deputy ....Naple of ....Gadsden County. Three witnesses have testified that these two officers carried Leroy from his mother's house about 11:30 that night, and the boy has not been seen or heard of since. Affidavits to this effect were submitted to Governor Caldwell, but no action has been taken.

In only one of these cases (Sam McFadden) has anyone been arrested or convicted. Even in this case the Suwannee County Grand Jury refused to return an indictment, and Federal authorities could move only under a weak civil rights statute. Thus a man gets off with only a year in jail and a fine of $1000 for committing first degree murder. In the other cases mentioned above the officers were not even suspended for their failure to protect the helpless prisoners entrusted to their care.

We cannot afford to wait until the several states get "trained" or "educated" to the point where they can take effective action in such cases. Human life is too valuable for mere experimenting of this kind. The Federal Government must be empowered to take the necessary action for the protection of its citizens. We need a Federal law with "teeth". We therefore urge you to work for the passage of the Wagner-.... Morse-Case Bill during this session of Congress.

Respectfully yours,
Harry T. Moore, Executive Secretary

Florida State Conference, NAACP
Progressive Voters' League of Florida, Inc.

There was a never-ending cycle of black victims from white terror in Florida and Harry was determined to make people listen.

But many blacks were too frightened to testify in courtroom trials; eyewitnesses suddenly had amnesia; African American ministers and preachers often pleaded with Harry to quit stirring up 'the hornet's nest'. Their advice was: "just get along".

Anyone who did cooperate with law enforcement to testify against racially-motivated crimes was either threatened or killed. And if blacks did cooperate, with whom could they feel safe to offer evidence or testimony?

So many officers of the court and a large percentage of law enforcement officers were members of the Ku Klux Klan or sympathetic. And if ever one of these officers were questioned or charged with any improprieties they would cover for each other. The 'deck was stacked' against blacks at every turn.

It was a desperately dangerous environment.

Soon Harry T. Moore established a working relationship with the formidable NAACP lawyer, Thurgood Marshall, who would later become a renowned Supreme Court Justice. Marshall and Moore worked closely together on criminal cases. Often Marshall could be found sleeping over in the Moore home on the sofa while preparing legal cases for the NAACP.

REQUESTING COUNSEL TO THURGOOD MARSHALL

Florida State conference of the National Association
for the Advancement of Colored People
Mims, Fla

June 30, 1944

Attorney Thurgood Marshall, Special Counsel
69 Fifth Ave., New York, N. Y.

Dear Attorney Marshall:

As you know, the Suwannee County, Fla. Grand Jury last month failed
to indict the three white men accused of lynching Willie James Howard
on Jan. 2. Frankly, we expected this negative decision from a state jury,
but we followed the advice of Gov. Holland and your office and helped
to arrange for the father to return to Live Oak for the hearing.

Apparently, the local officials, especially the sheriff, were reluctant to
prosecute this case. It seems that the sheriff was very much upset when
he learned that Mr. Howard actually was there to testify. We are forced
to wonder if the sheriff himself is not involved in this crime. It is very
probable that he at least has tried to help cover up the facts in this case.
For your information we are inclosing copy of the father's statement,
telling just what happened during the hearing.

We are wondering now if there is any chance for further action in Federal
Court. Both the Orange County Branch and the State Conference are
anxious that every possible action be taken to secure justice in this case.
And, as you perhaps know, a branch of the NAACP has been organized
at Live Oak. We are ready to throw our financial support to any further
effort that might bring the guilty parties to justice.

Please let us have your opinion in this matter.

Very sincerely yours,
Harry T. Moore

Harry complained, vehemently, against segregated schools, lynchings, and deficient salaries for black teachers. His confronting the School Board for their underpaying black teachers combined with his political activities were too much for the School Board. Both Harry and Harriette were fired from their teaching positions in 1946.

After their termination, Harry and his family devoted themselves full-time to their activist duties. Harriette and their two daughters, Evangeline and Annie, were engulfed in Harry's activities.

They spoke at public events, his daughters recited text they had rehearsed to educate the black community, and the team of Harriette with Evangeline and Annie coordinated his trips across the state, wrote letters, and managed many administrative duties to advance the cause. They were a team.

JUANITA BARTON INTERVIEW (CONT'D)

GREGORY: Harry Moore was gaining momentum. He seemed to be developing a real political force but was he fully supported by the black community?

JUANITA: In those days you didn't know who you could trust. You know it's one thing to accuse a KKK member or a policeman or a corrupt lawyer, but in the black community, we found many occasions where we'd be talking to an individual... he could be a dockworker or a fisherman or even a lawyer who would be black, and he would say they weren't in support of what Harry was doing because he was rocking the boat. They didn't want to see their positions jeopardized or some punishment levied against the community because of Harry's actions, so they would not support him.

GREGORY: What would they do?

JUANITA: All they had to do was fire you because there was always somebody looking for a job. A part of it was fear, absolutely, but a part of it was economics, as well. You make a choice, and at least you don't want to cross the line. Maybe you don't do anything actively that's in any way going to stop Harry, but you maybe don't cooperate with him or don't advocate what he advocates, and that's what's important. It isn't just a black or white issue. It's a complicated political, economic, personal issue on all levels.

Harry traveled to churches, schools, and any public forums available, to teach blacks about voter registration. Once registered, he assembled black votes into voting blocks and made sure they were systematically applied in elections as 'block votes.'

This method gave African Americans potential political sway in Florida's elections. They couldn't win an election, but they could cause an upset. His work was having an effect. In the eyes of the 'white' establishment, Harry T. Moore was fast becoming a political threat. And he was not yet finished finding new ways to confront the white bureaucracy.

Harry was about to go head-to-head with some of the most dangerous adversaries in the state in Central Florida over the soon-to-be-infamous Groveland Four.

THE BOMB HEARD AROUND THE WORLD

Repercussions from Florida blast make it most explosive since Hiroshima atom bomb.

Reprinted from a 1952 EBONY (EBONY November, 1975)

The BOMB went off with a deafening roar at 10:20 on Christmas night. Neighbors thought it was a Christmas firecracker. But, the next morning they awoke to discover that the most explosive bomb since Hiroshima had been detonated in the midst of their quiet orange groves.

Dead was Harry T. Moore, head of Florida's NAACP. Dying was his wife, Harriet.

A white man who came to see the wreckage of the little frame cottage where the Moore's lived remarked: "That's one coon who will keep his mouth shut."

Moore's mouth was indeed shut forever. But, the bomb that rocked his home and took his life was heard around the world.

Echoes of the explosion reverberated from Rangoon to Rio, from Moscow to Mexico City until the blast in the little Florida town of Mims (pop. 1,081) became the most publicized since the atom bomb was dropped on Japan.

Its toll was only two people, a shy, graying, scholarly school teacher and his wife , but the symbolic significance of their deaths was world wide in its import. Harry Tyson Moore was a man who ground out handouts about equal education on his mimeograph machine in his small six-room cottage, drove his new Buick around the state to talk about civil rights and attended NAACP meetings where he became so active he was named state head of the organization. He was killed for that.

The world quickly took note. In Asia and Africa, Moore's slaying in a nation that called itself the world's greatest democracy became front page news. Newspapers in France and Brazil, in Israel and the Philippines editorialized about the death of Moore. In the world forum of the United Nations, Russia's foreign Minister Andrei Vishinsky was quick to throw the Moore murder in the faces of American delegates, including one Negro delegate, Channing Tobias. Behind the iron curtain, the Communists had a field day with dispatches from the Russian Tass news agency with details of the Moore slaying.

America's foremost delegate to the UN, Eleanor Roosevelt, admitted: "That kind of violent incident will be spread all over every country in the world and the harm it will do us among the people of the world is untold."

Over decent Americans, a pall of shame settled. More sermons were preached, more resolutions adopted and more protest telegrams and letters sent about the Moore killing than about any other racial event in a decade. America accepted the castigation of the world and vowed that it would try to do better.

The bomb and its world repercussions symbolized dramatically a new era in U. S. Race relations. For today America can no longer say that its race problem is its own affair. The bomb demonstrated conclusively that U. S. Racists must answer to a new judge and jury, world opinion.

Governor Adlai Stevenson succinctly stated the new concept in an address to the National Urban League when he said: "The ramparts of democracy are not only in Korea nor along the Western European defense line, they are in Cicero, in Miami and Birmingham."

FLORIDA OFFERS $2,000 REWARD IN BOMBING OF NEGRO'S HOME

The Christian Science Monitor
Associated Press - 12/27/51
Mims, Florida

The State of Florida has offered a $2,000 reward in the fatal bombing of a prominent Negro leader. At the same time, his injured wife said she had "a couple of ideas" as to who might be responsible. Federal, state, and Brevard County officials were probing the case with unannounced results as to what kind of bomb it was or who might have set it off.

But this was generally accepted: The reason Harry T. Moore was slain and his wife hurt in the blast which shattered their isolated home near here Christmas night was his aggressive leadership in state Negro affairs. Gov. Fuller Warren said he would pay $2,000 for information bring about conviction of those responsible for the bombing and another $1,000 for information leading to conviction of those guilty of bombing and leaving explosives near Jewish, Negro, and Roman Catholic centers in Dade County (Miami).

In a Sanford hospital Mrs. More told a newspaper report: "I have a couple of ideas who might have done it, but when people do those kind of things, they have someone else do it." Then she added: "I was asleep at the time and didn't see anything."

Leaders of the National Association for Advancement of Colored People in New York immediately said there was a connection between the Christmas night bombing and the widely known Groveland rape case and a series of attacks directed at Jews, Roman Catholics, and Negroes in Florida since last June.

Mary McLeod Bethune, president-emeritus of Bethune-Cookman College for Negroes at Daytona Beach, said Mr. Moore had spoken at several Florida meetings in connection with the Groveland case, and added: I think possibly the aggressiveness of Mr. Moore in pointing out to Negroes the opportunities of true citizenship may have been a reason."

A student at Sarah Lawrence College was deeply concerned by the bombing of the Moore family. She wrote to President Truman.

Mr. P. Nash

To file

1/23

Sarah Lawrence College - Bronxville, New York   January 21, 1952

FILE - M.W.

Dear Mr. Truman,

I am a student at Sarah Lawrence College, and for the past eight or nine years, my schooling has emphasized principles that our country stands for — freedom to think and act as an individual, equality for all men, protection for the citizen to maintain his ideals. I cannot help but feel puzzled when I read about such incidents as the murder of Harry T. Moore and his wife. Is our philosophy of action different from the high ideals which we advocate?

It seems to me that the course that we, as a nation standing for freedom & equality for all men, must take is to persue the ruthless undemocratic men who killed this citizen for

continued on next page

Sarah Lawrence College - Bronxville, New York

trying to assert the natural
rights of his people. These
men should be apprehended and
punished, as a living example
that the United States not only
preaches high moral values, but
lives and acts by Her own
dictates & principles.

        Sincerely,

            (Miss) Arden Rappaport

"To have a couple blown up in their own home, on their anniversary, on Christmas Day, you can't write that. It's a reality that's stunning in its drama, and to not have it resolved sooner than we were able to resolve it is sad."

∼ Congressman Charlie Crist

Chapter 3

WHITE HOUSE AND
GLOBAL REACTIONS

Each of the Florida lynchings and the many other egregious racial injustices received considerable national press and began to reflect poorly on Florida's endeavors to shed its racist and violent image.

Historically, Florida had one of the worst track records in America where lynching was concerned. With the rapid growth of a post-war industry, Floridians had hoped to depict the state as a modern and forward-thinking society. It was not the case.

After the death of the Moores in Mims, Florida's long legacy of violence continued to plague the state. And there were more bombings, not only of blacks but of Jews and Catholics, too. According to White House sources, by March 1952, over six thousand cards arrived in the mailroom regarding the bombing of Harry T. Moore.

The death toll was two people, but the symbolic significance of their deaths was worldwide in its notoriety and importance.

Harry Moore was a man in a small town, in a tiny home, who printed handouts on an old Ditto machine. However, the bomb that killed him and its global repercussions produced an alternative view of American race relations and its global perception.

The Moore assassinations triggered many countries to 'sound off' on America's questionable values and many hypocrisies. The assassinations rapidly turned into an international incident.

America had, before, during, and after World War ll, proudly touted liberty, human rights, equality, and opportunity for all. It bragged of its record as an iconic beacon for the future of humankind.

The reality was otherwise.

In Asia and Africa, on the front page of newspapers, Harry and Harriette Moore's slaying was seen as a lie coming from a nation that called itself "the

Eleanor Roosevelt

world's greatest democracy." Newspapers in Israel, Brazil, France, and the Philippines, harshly criticized America's brutal track record.

If this is the best America has to offer then it's certainly not good enough, most countries pronounce in the press.

Harry Moore lived in a society where "Jim Crow" beliefs were a driving force in America's consciousness, and lynchings were an everyday event most Americans wanted to ignore - much as Jews in Germany were persecuted and ultimately ignored in Nazi Germany -- until it was too late.

Comparisons were undeniable in 1951 with the recent conclusion of World War ll and its holocaust in recent memory.

Regardless, the assassinations of Harry and Harriette Moore were quickly and eagerly forgotten by a society unwilling to acknowledge its apathy and ignorance.

It appeared that America, because of its inability to take effective action was offering tacit approval for the outrageous behavior of the Moore assassination and other such racially-motivated crimes inflicted on African Americans. The Moore murders were the 12th racial bombing in Florida in 1951.

Still, others, who were sympathetic to the Moores and what they stood for, were afraid of American law enforcement and government to provide information or evidence which could have been helpful in prosecuting racially-motivated crimes.

After all, many in law enforcement and government were actual members of the KKK or, at least sympathetic to their racist beliefs. Repercussions from Florida blast made this and over a dozen or more other bombings the most controversial since the Hiroshima atomic bomb.

Comparisons were undeniable in 1951

*Many in law enforcement and government were actual members
of the KKK or at least sympathetic to their racist beliefs.*

Chapter 4
GROVELAND

LAKE COUNTY FLORIDA - 1949

In 1949, four young African Americans were charged with the rape of a white woman. Two of the four blacks were arrested quickly. The remaining two would meet their fates soon after. The four young black men were Charles Greenlee, Samuel Shepherd, Walter Irvin, and Ernest Thomas.

The arrests and charges against the four were, at very least, questionable. Sheriff McCall and his law enforcement methods were undeniably racist, violent, illegal, and disregarded due process to a level of criminality.

Not only was there a lack of evidence, but there were no reliable witnesses, and no actual proof the girl had ever been accosted or raped. The medical examiner could find no evidence of sexual contact, bruises, or any indication of the alleged crime.

As well, there were witnesses indicating that one of the defendants, Walter Irvin, was in a different town when the alleged rape occurred. From a law enforcement perspective, everything that could be done wrong was.

Once Harry Moore learned of this, he jumped into action. The clock was ticking. In this part of Florida, (which was dominated by white supremacists and Jim Crow methods) these black defendants might never survive long enough to defend themselves in a trial.

It was clear that information gathered pointed to a racially-motivated excuse to infuse fear into the black population, and denying any semblance of due process was an ideal tool.

At this time in Florida, the sentence for a black man who had raped a white woman was the death penalty. White law enforcement officials were motivated to have four black defendants executed. The honor of 'white women' must be respected. Cries for revenge echoed loudly across Florida.

Willis V. McCall had been a fruit and vegetable inspector for Florida. In

PROGRESSIVE VOTERS' LEAGUE OF FLORIDA

INCORPORATED

Mims, Florida
December 2, 1951

Governor Fuller Warren
State Capitol
Tallahassee, Florida

Dear Governor :

Sane-minded Florida citizens of all classes, creeds and colors must be shocked over recent developments in the famous Groveland Case. Despite the report of the coroner's jury that Sheriff McCall acted "in line of duty" when he shot Shepherd and Irvin, those fateful shots fired near Weirsdale on the night of Nov. 6th are still echoing around the world.

Thinking people naturally ask these questions : (1) In view of the mob action directed against these prisoners in 1949, was it safe to transport them into Lake County again with a guard of only two officers ? (2) Did Sheriff McCall use sound judgement in attempting to drive his car and guard two prisoners at the same time ? (3) Why did the officers follow a "blind" clay road after leaving Weirsdale ? (4) If the prisoners did try to escape (which is extremely doubtful), was it necessary to shoot them four times in order to stop them, especially when they were handcuffed together ? (5) Since the three Groveland Boys had complained of severe beatings and inhuman treatment by Lake County officers in 1949, why were they permitted to leave Raiford again in custody of these same officers ? (6) Is it true that in Florida the word of a Negro means nothing when weighed against that of a white person (as indicated by the three prisoners' complaints in 1949 and by Irvin's sworn statement last month) ? (7) In the face of such strong evidence of gross neglect or wilful intent to murder the prisoners, why have these officers not been suspended ?

Yes, these questions are too important to be ignored. We need not try to "whitewash" this case or bury our heads in the sand, like an ostrich. Florida is on trial before the rest of the world. Only prompt and courageous action by you in removing these officers can save the good name of our fair state. We also repeat our request for ample and constant State guard for Irvin in future hearings on this case.

Florida Negro citizens are still mindful of the fact that our votes proved to be your margin of victory in the 2nd primary of 1948. We seek no special favors; but certainly we have a right to expect justice and equal protection of the laws even for the humblest Negro. Shall we be disappointed again ?

Respectfully yours,

Harry T. Moore, Executive Secretary
Progressive Voters' League of Florida

Fuller Warren Papers, Box 53
Florida State Archives

*"Harry Moore wrote to Governor Fuller about the shootings
and the injustice of the Groveland Case."*

February 1944 the former Sheriff passed away, and McCall ran for the job. His pitch in the campaign was that he could not be bought.

Said McCall, "my only promise is a good, clean, fearless and conscientious execution of my duties. I know, and my friends know I am strong enough to resist the temptation to sell my trust for profit." He won the job.

Sheriff Willis McCall quickly became 'the muscle' for the white men who owned citrus companies. He was a dedicated loyalist, racist and segregationist. And he was proud of it.

McCall knew how to make his base happy. Citrus growers wanted a big bully to keep their black workers in line. He did so with zeal.

On July 17, 1949. Seventeen-year old Norma Padgett and her husband, Willie, offered their 'rape and kidnapping' story to Sheriff McCall.

McCall immediately picked up two (potential) black suspects; he only needed two more to round out her story.

A few days later, a vigilante posse roamed the countryside, intent on avenging the honor of their women. Locals were 'out for blood' now. Righteous indignation had infected the white residents. And Ku Klux Klansmen suddenly appeared en masse. Cars filled with enraged whites raced through the streets, while groups of bitter white men gathered to collectively dole out retribution.

To halt a potential race war in Lake County, Governor Fuller Warren, mobilized the National Guard as more Klansmen converged from all over Florida and Georgia, too. It was a deadly situation which could erupt at any moment.

The Ku Klux Klan distributed hand-outs to the white population:

"THIS IS A WHITE MAN'S ORGANIZATION exalting the Caucasian race and teaching the doctrine of white supremacy. This does not mean that we are enemies of the colored and mongrel races. But it does mean that we are organized to establish the solidarity and to realize the mission of the white race. "

There it was. The Fugitive Slave Act and the Supreme Court's Plessy vs. Ferguson Decision were still alive and operating in 1949. Ninety-nine years earlier, in 1850, and fifty-three year earlier, in 1896, respectively. the

ATL228-7/21-TAVARES, FLA: Willie Padgett and his wife, Norma, victim of an alleged rape-rob attack by four Negroes last week, relax with a soft-drink after a session of questioning by State's Attorney J. W. Hunter. Hunter said he would ask for indictments charging the Negroes with rape, armed robbery, and kidnapping. CREDIT (ACME TELEPHOTO)

government in Washington, D. C. passed laws allowing white Americans to claim blacks who might be runaway slaves, solely based on a white pursuer's say, while Plessy vs. Fergusson declared segregation as a core value of American society. This was the invention of "separate but equal' in an alleged democracy.

Meanwhile Lake County, citrus company owners feared any visitors from the North who might instill unhealthy ideas in their black citrus workers. If any one person or group spoke of organizing a 'union' they would be putting their lives at risk. White company owners used fear as the motivation to hold down black workers; keep them quiet, cooperative, working hard, working cheaply, and subservient. They wouldn't tolerate unions or runaways. So they used every avenue possible to keep a tight reign on their workers.

There are amendments to the U.S. Constitution which address equality, rights, freedom, liberty. But that's only on paper. None of this applied to blacks. African Americans had no rights, no recourse, no due process, and they had no active constitutional rights to defend themselves. Supreme Court decisions throughout American history made sure of this.

Locals in Lake County already knew what the Klan stood for. The influence of the Klan touched every facet of life: government, law enforcement, justice, religion, education, and commerce. An army of Klansmen merged with five hundred armed locals who lined the streets by the time fifty Lake County National Guardsmen arrived.

The white mob (of over two hundred whites) began their rampage. They burned, pillaged, and attacked black families. They set fire to black-owned

Sheriff McCall with Norma and Willie Padgett

homes. Black families sprinted into the groves and forests around the city, terrified and defenseless.

Sheriff Willis V. McCall did nothing to halt the mob. And no one was ever charged for these attacks. Ironically, both Walter Irvin and Samuel Shepherd, two of the defendants in the Groveland case, had served honorably in the U.S. Army in the Korean War. They had been members of the 453rd Signal Heavy Construction Company, U.S. Army Air Corps before returning home. Other than minor infractions, none of the four defendants had ever committed any crimes which reflected the current accusations on deck.

Nearly one thousand whites raced through the groves and surrounding forest to track the last 'rapist.' They tracked him with dogs through the night, through swamps, and lakes. They were determined.

Soon Ernest R. Thomas was cornered and killed by the posse. They shot him multiple times. A hearing ruled he was lawfully killed trying to escape. Rumors surfaced that he had been slaughtered. Reports allege he had nearly four hundred bullets in his body. The source for this number of bullets was never revealed.

NAACP attorney, Thurgood Marshall, was horrified. He demanded an investigation. "This wanton killing by a deputized mob is worse than a lynching," Marshall charged.

Lake County's white population met their returning sheriff as a conquering hero, while Harry T. Moore started his process of writing to the Governor, the NAACP, and the media. He was now fully engaged.

By engaging in battle with Sheriff McCall, Harry T. Moore and his family entered the cross-hairs of the Ku Klux Klan and the many corrupt officials with whom they were associated. Indeed, many officials or participants in the Groveland case were active members of the Ku Klux Klan. And if they were not members, or had relatives who were, many were, at very least, sympathetic to their cause.

Harry T. Moore was not intimidated nor would he going to let fear guide him. He immediately sent a wire to Governor Fuller Warren demanding that Sheriff McCall be held accountable for the racial unrest in Groveland. But Governor Warren was not so sympathetic where matters of race were concerned.

On winning the governorship, Governor Fuller Warren denounced the Klan:

"The hooded hoodlums and sheeted jerks who paraded the streets of Tallahassee last night made a disgusting and alarming spectacle. These covered cowards who call themselves Klansmen quite obviously have set out to terrorize minority groups in Florida, as they have in a near-by State."

However, Governor Fuller Warren's track record was, at very least, checkered in this area. Upon being discovered, Governor Warren had to admit that he had been a former member of the Ku Klux Klan, himself.

Harry Moore wired the Governor. *(below)*

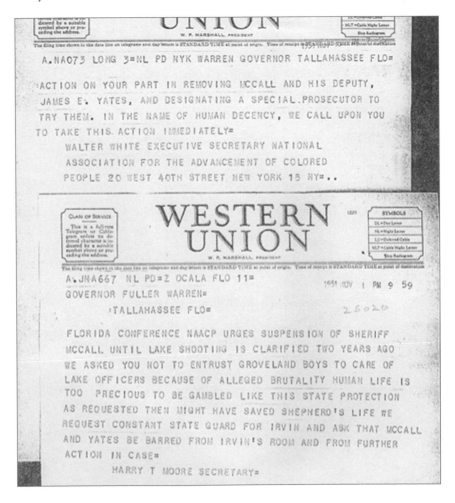

BOMBING CLIMAXED
SERIES OF OUTRAGES

Reprinted from 1952 EBONY (EBONY November, 1975)

RACE VIOLENCE in Florida flared often during the past year, but it took the bomb murder of Florida NAACP leader Harry T. Moore to focus worldwide attention on violence in the state.

Racial tension in the state has been building up ever since four Negro youths were arrested in Lake County in 1949 and charged with the rape of a young white housewife. One of the youths was killed by a posse, the three others were tried and one was given life while Samuel Shepherd and Walter Lee Irvin, both 23, were sentenced to death. The NAACP led a fight to free the condemned men and the U. S. Supreme Court reversed the decision. Death entered the picture again when Sheriff Willis V. McCall killed Shepherd and wounded Irvin, claiming they had tried to escape while being taken to Tavares for a court hearing. Known as the "Groveland Case" and "The Little Scottsboro Case," the trails and the "legal murder" stirred up strong feelings both among Negroes and whites.

The Groveland Case was but one incident in a series of violent racial incidents during 1951. Prior to the lynching of Melvin Womack, another Negro, Willie Vincent, had been beaten by three white men and tossed from a speeding car with a fractured skull. In the same area, Luther Coleman, a Negro janitor at the Winter Garden elementary school, was beaten up by white men and a teen-age shoe shine boy, Jimmy Woodards, was shot five times but recovered.

Moore spoke out against the floggings and beatings. He was interested in the Groveland case and campaigned for the prosecution of the sheriff that shot the two Negro youths in the case. Moore was well thought of by most whites in the area. One business-man in nearby Orlando, who had known Moore in political work, said Moore was a "level-headed man with a deep feeling for his people. Moore wasn't an extremist. He wasn't a rabble-rouser."

Quiet and controlled as they were, Moore's speeches and his activities were enough to enflame many Southern whites against him. When he and his wife retired on Christmas night after a ham and turkey dinner with his mother, his daughter Annie, and his wife's brother, M/Sgt. George Simms, who had just returned from Korea, it was just a little after 10 p.m. The family had not opened their Christmas presents for they were waiting for Moore's daughter, Evangeline, to come home from Washington, D. C.

Moore never got to see what was in the gaily-wrapped packages. About ten minutes after the lights were turned out in the Moore cottage, someone placed a powerful explosive (probably nitroglycerine) under the bedroom floor and the blast fatally injured both Moore and his wife.

Chapter 5

INTERNATIONAL RESPONSE TO THE GROVELAND FOUR CASE

Sheriff McCall with defendants Charles Greenlee, Walter Irvin and Samuel Shepherd

The national publicity that grew out of the Groveland trial and the subsequent attempts to appeal to both the state and Supreme Courts indicated the changing domestic and international attitudes toward racial violence in America.

Following the end of World War II, the issue of race catapulted the United States onto the international scene.

Speaking to the United Nations General Assembly, Andrei Vishinsky, the chief Soviet delegate, commented on the Groveland murders by remarking that the United States "had a nerve talking about human rights and upbraiding other nations while Negroes were shot down by an officer of law while in custody."

Defendants Walter Irvin and Sam Shepherd with Thurgood Marshall

With the mention of McCall's shooting of Shepherd during the proceedings of the United Nations, even in the context of a jab of one country against another, it is evident that the world had changed.

'Jim Crow' was casting a hypocritical shadow over the upright image of democracy. As America became a dominant world power, discrepancies and policies that might have gone unnoticed before the war were now greatly magnified on the world stage.

In Paris, a highly-regarded black crusader, William L. Patterson, head of the Civil Rights Congress, leveled a charge of 'genocide' against the Government of the United States, charging it with responsibility for the murder of hundreds of thousands of Negroes.

The eyes of the world were on Florida and America. Attention was being paid to African American ghettoes, police brutality, racial injustice, racially-skewed laws against black Americans, segregation, unemployment, meager wages, and lynchings.

Was this the real America, they asked?

The three young men, (one only 16 years old), were found guilty by an all-white jury. The judge sentenced the youngest, Charles Greenlee, to life in prison while Sam Shepherd and Walter Irvin were sentenced to death.

This was Walter Irvin's explanation of the events surrounding the alleged crime. *(shown on opposite page)*

Charles Greenlee, Walter Irvin, and Samuel Shepherd, were convicted of rape despite dubious evidence and a highly-prejudiced trial were found guilty by an all-white jury. Much evidence was excluded or disallowed during the trial while witnesses and experts were intimidated or threatened.

Much of the testimony (including the Medical Examiner's) would likely have exonerated them. The Medical Examiner's conclusion was that there was no proof Norma Padgett was ever raped.

And there were eyewitnesses confirming Walter Irvin was in another town at the time of the alleged crime. Harry Moore was enraged by this travesty and pressed for immediate action.

In the South, local and state governments sought to grapple with what appeared to be the beginnings of the rise of black resistance. And whites could not understand long-silent blacks suddenly, almost from nowhere, refusing to compromise on racial issues. White Southerners found it easier to blame outsiders than to accept that "their" blacks might find segregation unbearable. At least this was their misguided notion.

*Said Harry: "I'm going to keep doing it,
even if it costs me my life...I may live to be
a ripe old age or I may be killed tomor-
row, or next month, or perhaps never, but I
intend to do this until the day I die."*

∼ Harry T. Moore

My name is Walter Ervin. I am twenty-two Years old. I was living in Grover, Florida with my mother, father, three little brothers and one sister. Sammie Shepard, a friend of mine came to my house in his brothers car in a mercury and picked me up about 9:00 at night, but I am not sure about the time. We went and got some gasoline and put into the car at Clermont at a gas station the name of which I donnot remember, but I can show you where it is.

Then we drove to Orlando. We went down on Church Street. We didn't do anything, just talked to some girls. We had a beer a piece, but I don't know whether it was in Orlando or somewhere else. It was not in Orlando I think. I don't remember exactly what time we left Orlando, but I know it wasn't late when I got back home. We left Orlando, and Sammie dropped me off at home and I went in the house and went to bed. Next morning I had got up and put on these same pants (blue jeans) I had on a pair of rubber shoes and before I had a chance to wash up, three or four car loads of policemans came up to the house most of them had on some kind of uniforms, but one or two wore plain clothes. The cops came up in front my house right behind my brother in law in the same car that we had been driving the night before. They were talking to my brother in law. One of the men not in uniform said something to Sammie who had got out of my brother in laws car and made an attempt to hit him and said that the son of a bitch, I remember that son of a bitch. Pretty soon the policeman called me out there and told me to get in the car, my mother begin crying. They did not do anything to me in front of the house. They drove out in the woods with me and Sammie, all the cars came along. We were both in the same car. I have never seen any one of these policemen before. There is only one policeman that I know of around Groveland and he was not there.

They drove out and parked along the woods on clay road, told us to get out of the car boy. I didn't see who grabbed Sammie, but one short guy in plain clothes who had a pistol belt grabbed me and hit me with his billy a lot of times across the head. He held me, and a lot of the others started to hitting me with billies and fist, and knocking me down and kicking me and picking me up and knocking me down again. This went on for about twenty minutes. When they were beating me, they said to me: "Nigger, you the one that picked up this white girl last night." I said to them what white girl? They said "well you might as well tell us, youre the one did it cause we gonna beat the hell out of you until you tell us you did do it." I still told them I was not the one. As far as I remember I always told them I was not the one. When they beat me up they pushed me into the car like that (jesture) I was bleeding pretty bad mostly from my head. They had me hand cuffed all this time and made sit up on the edge of the seat of the car to keep from getting blood on the seat. They taken us to the County jail in Tavares. They put us in a big cell with some more guys. This was still morning-I don't have any idea what time. They let us stay in the cell a while and then they came back and taken us down in the hole of a jail.

(Signed) W.I.

As Executive Director of the NAACP Harry Moore immediately organized a campaign against the wrongful convictions of the three men. He raised money for their appeals and contacted NAACP Attorney, Thurgood Marshall, to enlist his services.

With Thurgood's and Harry's support, backed by the NAACP, appeals were successful.

By April 1951 a legal team, headed by Thurgood Marshall, won the appeal for Shepherd's and Irvin's convictions before the U.S. Supreme Court.

Lake County Sheriff Willis V. McCall and his Deputy Leroy Campbell

While in the custody of Sheriff Willis McCall and awaiting their first trial, all three defendants were brutally beaten and tortured in the Lake County Jail. Following the reversal of their convictions, Sherriff McCall volunteered to personally transport two of the men back to the Lake County Jail from Florida State Prison for retrial. En route to the jail, on November 6, 1951, McCall shot Shepherd and Irvin.

McCall claimed that his prisoners, handcuffed to each other in the back of the police car, attempted to attack him when he stopped on a deserted road to check his car tires. McCall shot both men.

Shepherd died instantly from his wounds. Deputy James Yates, who was summoned to the scene, observed that Mr. Irvin was wounded but still alive,

Sheriff Willis McCall after shooting Samuel Shepherd & Walter Irvin while being transported to Lake County (State Archives of Florida) (1951)

Walter Irvin and Samuel Shepherd shot by Sheriff McCall

and shot him once more in the neck. Yates and McCall then ripped McCall's clothing and struck a blow to his head to substantiate his self-defense claims.

After multiple parties arrived at the scene, someone observed that Mr. Irvin was miraculously still alive, and he ultimately survived his injuries. Though Mr. Irvin told the NAACP and the FBI that McCall had shot him and Mr. Shepherd without cause, a white coroner's jury found that McCall had acted in self-defense and cleared his name.

Walter Irvin survived his gunshot wounds and later testified that Sheriff McCall shot them both in cold blood. McCall remained Lake County Sheriff until 1972 when he was indicted for the murder of yet another black prisoner.

After the shootings, Harry Moore called for legal action against Sheriff Willis McCall and his deputy, calling on Florida Governor Fuller Warren to suspend McCall and arrest them both for murder. Harry Moore's plea for justice was ignored.

Samuel Shepherd (killed by Sheriff McCall)

In the Appeal, the surviving defendants were found guilty a second time. The jurisdiction where the second trial was adjudicated was considered one of the most racist in Florida.

Remarkably, the same judge was used for both trials. And Sheriff Willis McCall was never charged with shooting Samuel Shepherd.

GARY CORSAIR INTERVIEW (CONT'D)

GREGORY: Harry Moore stood up to Sheriff McCall and then he called for McCall's arrest after he shot Samuel Shepherd and Walter Irvin.

GARY: Yes. What was amazing about Harry T. Moore is that he knew exactly what he was dealing with. And yet he bravely pressed on because it was the right thing to do. The Groveland Four needed representation and he was primarily responsible for Thurgood Marshall coming aboard (to represent them) for the retrial. When I got the families of the Groveland defendants together and they looked through my files, the one thing I kept hearing from them was, "We had no idea. We didn't know this happened to our relatives." And it really impressed upon me that if you were black in 1951 and an injustice was committed against you, you had no recourse. You shut your mouth and you were more careful in the future.

GREGORY: And Harry Moore?

GARY: He knew he was playing with fire. He'd been followed many times before. He'd been threatened before - but that man was just so courageous, fearless.

GREGORY: I read a newspaper an interview where he said, "I don't think I'm gonna be around a long time. I think, eventually, they're gonna get me."

GARY: That is exactly what he said. And he had to know with Groveland that when he stuck his nose in it, and Sheriff Willis McCall would retaliate. Harry needed to mind his own business and let Lake County take care of Lake County. He knew he offended the wrong guy and there could only be one outcome. But I don't think it mattered to him. In a way, I think he was proud and willing to die for his cause.

GREGORY: Why was his belief system so strong, do you think?

GARY: I think he had just seen so much of it. I think he reached a boiling point. His sense of justice and fair play was obviously absolutely off the charts. From what I learned, he was an exceptional human being. But here's what I always say: without Harry T. Moore there would be no story of the Groveland Four, because those young men wouldn't have survived that weekend (after they were arrested). They would have been swinging from trees or they would have been thrown off a bridge. But the fact that Harry T. Moore jumped on it and got it in the papers right away saved them. Lake County couldn't murder the three Groveland defendants because Harry turned the spotlight on it so quickly.

～

Chapter 6
FLORIDA TERROR

To look at Harry T. Moore, only, would be an error. The context of his actions is crucial to understanding the many moving parts at play in Florida and in America.

Many incendiary events occurred in Florida at this time. And the press in Florida had coined a brand new phrase in newspapers across the state. During the latter part of 1951, the media announced something new.

There were banner headlines with these words: "FLORIDA TERROR".

Commencing in 1951 there had been over a dozen racism-motivated bombings in different cities throughout the state. Each bomb attack was focused on minority groups, including Jewish, Catholic, and African American schools, housing projects, synagogues, community centers, churches, even a white-owned ice-cream parlor (The Creamette) in Orlando. Its owner had refused to build a separate window to serve blacks. It seems the terrorists

"Here is an example of what the KKK wanted at The Creamette ice-cream parlor. The owner wouldn't do it."

(later indicated by law enforcement to be the Ku Klux Klan) did not want blacks being served from a 'whites only' window. They bombed the ice-cream parlor.

The KKK had even left their initials on the doors of locations which received their special gifts of dynamite. Sometimes they added Nazi Swastikas beside their KKK initials. It was a fact that obtaining dynamite was extremely easy in Florida. And with bombs being (supposedly) untraceable, it was the preferred and most cowardly way to instigate fear and domestic terror.

The Klan in Florida was particularly active and aggressive at this time in American history. Historically, little had ever been done to punish the KKK for their despicable behavior. The passivity of law enforcement and the judiciary for these crimes sent a clear message to Klan members. They took this as a sign that they were, to some degree, 'bulletproof'.

After all, many in positions of power were corrupted by KKK influence or a white-supremacist point of view.

The Governor of Florida in 1951, Fuller Warren, had been an active member of the KKK prior to taking office, so his pedigree was, at very least, questionable. And those operating within the white-dominated infrastructure of Florida had done almost nothing to halt or punish racial crimes. One might interpret (or at least the Klan did) that there was, practically speaking, a 'soft approval' for their terrorist actions.

The bed sheet brigade is bad enough, but the real threat to Americans and human rights today is the plain clothes Klux in the halls of government and certain black-robed Klux on court benches."

⌒ Stetson Kennedy, author of "The Klan Unmasked"

THE BOMBINGS

White residents were given notice at the Carver Village development. And it caused enormous repercussions when it was learned that Carver would become part of the black community. Racial hatred grew.

This was a transition moment in the growth of Miami. Black housing was growing and urbanization created pockets of the city which had to accommodate the realities of the growing populace.

And so it was bombed. The buildings which had been bombed, thus far were owned by blacks or Jews. In September 1952 two packets of dynamite were utilized to blow up Carver Village. There were three bombings at Carver Village over a period of three months. More bombings of other locations continued after that. Soon churches and synagogues were hit next.

These 'terrorist attacks' were also poised to halt the Jewish population from establishing a footprint in Florida. Ironically, reports indicated if white-supremacists had to pick Jews or blacks, most of the polls stated Jews were preferred.

The Florida bombings continued through 1952, after the Harry T. Moore bombing. "Florida Terror" reached critical mass.

Fontainebleau Bombing

Miami Hebrew School Bombing

Carver Village Bombing

Between 1951 and 1952 there were between twelve and eighteen bombings around the state. Law enforcement crime reports report different numbers. Twelve was the minimum reported.

The economy began to suffer. Fearful tourists were unwilling to spend their holiday dollars in Florida, and law enforcement came under intense pressure to halt the 'bomb-happy' perpetrators, no matter what.

Harry T. Moore Bombing

Governor Warren's questionable history with the Klan was doing him no favors politically and the State of Florida had earned a rogue reputation for lynchings, the Groveland Four, and its KKK leanings already. "Florida Terror" added insult to injury.

The image of progressive, sunny Florida took a shellacking on many levels. The bombings had to stop. Harry and Harriette died in the twelfth bombing. Approximately six more occurred in 1952 before they finally halted.

While Abraham Lincoln freed the slaves, the party of Lincoln had radically changed. Republicans were not the party which cared about the rights of blacks or any minorities at that time. So all of Harry Moore's registrations were geared toward recruiting votes for Democrats. Democrats supported many of the changes needed to build a genuinely democratic society.

Without protection or support, Harry T. Moore had continued his vigorous protests against lynchings, police brutality, injustice for blacks, the tainted criminal justice system, and a prejudiced judiciary. The entire system was corrupt and he had been willing to put himself at risk to halt the damage being done.

There were no levels of authority off limits to Harry T. Moore.

Chapter 7

ASSASSINATIONS

H arry T. Moore and his wife, Harriette, were assassinated 12 years before Medgar Evers, 14 years before Malcolm X, and 17 years before Dr. Martin Luther King Jr.

Many African Americans were murdered in every decade in America, but as a legitimate activist working for the NAACP to bring about change in America, Harry T. Moore was the first in a series of racial 'assassinations,' far ahead of his time.

The label of 'murder' is generally applied when referring to the deaths of Harry T. and Harriette V. Moore. However, the word 'assassination' is more precise and respectful, given the political and racial circumstances of this crime.

ASSASSINATION: refers to a prominent person or persons who, for political, religious, economic, or racial reasons is (are) killed by order of an insurgent or rogue group or individuals operating outside the law.

White supremacists are an infection in American society. Like any disease or virus, they seem to erupt in waves, depending on the country's administration at the time; and they never really go away. The 1950's was a volatile decade, as most are, and racism was a hot-button issue in profound transition. That white supremacists assassinated Harry and Harriette Moore is indicative of America's growing pains in this brutal era where activists and innocents were often caught in the crossfire.

American society has been infected for a very long time with ethnic, minority and religious prejudice. For centuries before America became a country, there had always been a no tolerance/no civil rights policy inflicted specifically on African Americans. Many minorities suffered similar treatment, including Native Indians, Jews, Catholics, Japanese, Chinese, gays or anyone who appeared different or offered a contrary view, or who were sympathetic or aligned with any of these.

Harry T. Moore knew he held no sway in America as a whole, but in the state

Medgar Evers

Malcolm X

Dr. Martin Luther King Jr.

of Florida, with every racial injustice that came to his attention, he made it his mission to 'shake up' the establishment as often as he could.

After he and his wife were assassinated, many in law enforcement (and in the general population), did not believe (or wish to) that there was any connection between the bombing of the Moore home and the dozen or more racially-motivated Florida Terror bombings which had occurred at that time.

To acknowledge race crimes in Florida as part of a pattern that included the Moore bombing was not something law enforcement and state government wanted to confirm.

State administrators were fearful of blacks reacting in anger to a level where rioting could occur. There had been many race riots in other cities across the nation since the end of World War ll and Miami was hoping not to incite one now.

The Moore bombing occurred within a series of terror bombings, all racially and minority motivated, for nearly a year. And law enforcement was still unable to establish a connection between the serial bombings they called "Florida Terror" and the Moore attack. The methodology was nearly identical, as were the targets, and with each bomb that exploded a message was sent for anyone of color or a minority.

If the Ku Klux Klan was responsible (as suggested by FBI reports) for the Florida Terror bombings, and every attack was race-related, there is a compelling reason to believe there could have been a tangible connection between the Moore bombing and the Florida Terror serial bombings. In fact, it would be improbable if there was not.

While a legitimate connection may or may not have existed, 'patterns of actions' are crucially important in solving serial crimes and 'the connecting of dots' must not be dismissed without intuitive, comprehensive, scientific, expert analysis.

However, crime investigation at this time in history was, by no means, thorough or consistent, and in the South many issues came into play which severely impacted results of law enforcement procedures and prosecutions. Issues like economics, race, prejudice, and politics were profoundly impactful and influenced the outcome of many an investigation.

The FBI and local law enforcement were never able to prove a connection between the Florida Serial bombings and the Harry T. Moore assassinations. And no one was ever prosecuted for either.

With the benefit of hindsight and comparative analyses, it appears (from an outsider's perspective) that deficient forensic science also harmed the investigations of the bombings in Florida in 1951 and 52. And there were serious factors which came into play including unjustified crime theories, uncooperative locals, civilian prejudice, investigatory missteps, white supremacist conspiratorial conduct, sympathetic racist locals, law enforcement prejudice, political prejudice, judicial prejudice, and fear of violent retaliation.

While the bombing perpetrators were never prosecuted, one truth was certain: Harry T. and Harriette V. Moore were killed in a race-motivated domestic terrorist attack.

VICTIM IN WAITING

Harry T. Moore knew he was 'a victim' waiting to happen for a very long time. He had been followed, humiliated, rejected, dismissed, fired and threatened so many times. There was no doubt in his mind as to risk factors.

To his credit and detriment, Harry's tenacity and intelligence made him a formidable adversary. Government officials and white supremacists (KKK) began to fear his political power in the black community, which only deepened their hatred.

But they had good reason to fear him. His outspoken criticism of systemic racism in the school board, law enforcement, government, news media, social services, voting booths, and the courts, earned him a 'troublemaker' title (white supremacists favor the word: 'uppity').

Harry protested every racial injustice of any note that occurred in Florida. And he waged letter-writing campaigns, held rallies, ran fundraising drives, and initiated lawsuits to protest police brutality, lynchings, prejudiced courtrooms, and unfair labor practices, all of which were victimizing blacks.

And labor practices (called 'peonage') was being used to take advantage of blacks in brutal fashion. It was another form of slavery but with a different label. The working conditions and salaries of black citrus workers in Florida were catastrophically awful. While whites didn't call it 'slavery' anymore, peonage was, for all intents and purposes, the same thing.

Peonage definition:

1. the condition or service of a peon

2. the practice of holding a person(s) in servitude or partial slavery to work off a debt or to serve a false penal sentence

The practice of peonage occurred mostly in southern states where black men (usually) were picked up for minor crimes (such as vagrancy) or other falsified charges, and upon being faced with heinous court fines, they were pressed into working for local company owners to pay off these fictitious fines. After that, these black men were trapped in a hideous cycle that was, for many, inescapable.

These men were cheap labor for local white bosses and company owners.

Harry T. Moore was determined to break open this corrupt social system. His involvement in the NAACP only deepened as he learned more about the status of blacks in Florida. In 1946 he was elected as the first, full time, paid Executive Secretary of the Florida state conference of the NAACP. He later became its Coordinator, too.

Harry took his Executive Secretary position seriously and, on NAACP letterhead, he launched a full-frontal attack on Florida law enforcement and Florida's legal system. He wrote letter after letter to then Governor Fuller Warren, the Florida Attorney General's Office, State Attorneys, law enforcement, and top government officials, to criticize, complain, debate, educate, and confront.

Harry left no issue untouched. He was determined to halt corruption. And though he was only a 'one-man show' for civil rights, his drive, tenacity, political skills, creativity, and intelligence were unquestionable.

But soon the white establishment realized that he was also dangerous.

Harry knew he was crossing 'over the line' with the powers-that-be. Threats against him were real. It was no secret; not a private thought he kept to himself. He confirmed these risks in newspaper interviews, in conversations with colleagues, and with his family. And he refused to halt his efforts.

Evangeline Moore, daughter of Harry and Harriette Moore, said "He knew that one day he would probably be killed, and we knew that. But it's something that you don't dwell on."

Harry stated many times to his mother and his wife, "It's worth it."

In 1949 we know that he became extremely aggressive in his attempt to intervene in the Groveland Four rape trial. At that time he demanded that the enormously popular, yet controversial, Sheriff Willis McCall of Lake County, Florida, be indicted for McCall's mishandling of the Groveland Four case and the criminal shootings of Walter Irvin and Samuel Shepherd.

Sheriff Willis McCall

Harry contacted Governor Fuller Warren, the Attorney General, and law enforcement many times to call for McCall's arrest.

He gave newspaper interviews attacking McCall, expressed objections as to the lack of due process, and offered his observations of the gross racial injustices in the Groveland Four case. And he enlisted the services of the renowned attorney from the NAACP, Thurgood Marshall to obtain an Appeal from the Supreme Court. In short, Harry T. Moore went to war with the system.

His frustrations with the state's mishandling of the Groveland case took him to the next level in civil activism. But it also exposed him to some of the most violent and hateful white supremacists in the country.

To make matters more dangerous, white citrus farm owners believed Harry was meeting with 'union organizers' to discuss organizing blacks working in the citrus industry. During the McCarthy era in the 1950's, anyone talking with unions organizers was instantly labeled 'a communist.'

Of course, this label was thrown around easily by those hoping to tarnish the reputations of anyone who would impact the 'bottom line' of their respective companies or for anyone perceived as 'liberal.'

Harry knew what issues mattered and how to maximize damage to those who would deny blacks quality of life. And now his voting efforts were beginning to have a real impact in both state and federal elections. His 'block voting' strategy started to influence elections.

Now the white establishment began to pay close attention. But ironically, in 1951, the NAACP voted to terminate his job. While he was incredibly clever with his local efforts, the NAACP began to complain that he was spending too much time building a voting block and not devoting enough time to NAACP activities.

Both the FBI and FDLE confirm that the NAACP felt Harry was not focused on their purpose. And they indicated that they were running into budgetary issues in Florida. They (allegedly) wanted a larger NAACP membership to justify Harry's salary. The accusation was that Harry had not been bringing in enough new members for the organization due to his extracurricular activities.

Some of this information may have substance, but regardless of the reasons, they halted paying Harry T. Moore's salary. And Harry and his family suffered. They had to survive with little or no financial support. Harry lost his teaching job, Harriette lost her teaching job, and the NAACP terminated his salary. Harriette eventually found a teaching job in another city to keep the family afloat.

Harry kept working without a salary.

THE STATE OF FLORIDA VERSUS THE FBI

In 1951, the day after Christmas, in the wee hours of a foggy morning, after the deadly explosion at the Moore home, the State Police were relieved of their duties, and the FBI assumed command of the Harry T. and Harriette V. Moore assassinations.

Local Brevard County Sheriff H. T. "Bill" Williams arrived with a dog handler and bloodhound after a call from Deputy Clyde Bates, who had reached the scene at 10:45 P.M., twenty-five minutes after the explosion.

Sheriff Williams was considered by many to be a good man. He had a decent reputation in both the white and the black communities and was also known to be honest and reliable; a rarity in law enforcement in Florida in that era.

The sheriff found the Moore home catastrophically damaged by the explosion. Every window in the house had been blown out, the entire length of the flooring had been ripped open; splintered pieces of wood had become

FBI with State Police

projectiles and embedded themselves in the rafters. The chimney had been lifted off the ground with the bomb's concussion also destroying every piece of furniture. The Moore's bedroom was blown apart from floor to ceiling.

Sheriff Williams immediately walked the property with his dog handler and bloodhound in search of usable evidence. The dog found footprints in the grove behind the house, under a thicket of orange trees. Unfortunately, most of the other footprints and potential evidence, had been contaminated by undisciplined local law enforcement and concerned, or otherwise fascinated on-lookers, traipsing around or through the crime scene.

Just after 3 A.M., the FBI arrived to take command of the investigation. Sheriff Williams and his officers were relieved of their duties.

Harry T. Moore had become an outspoken leader in a southern black community, and now the world was about to learn he had been assassinated in, what was likely, a white supremacist-motivated attack.

The FBI and Truman administration understood that news of the Moore killings was about to become volatile, high-profile, controversial, and politically-charged. Harry T. Moore, the Executive Secretary of the NAACP, was an official martyr.

But the FBI did not have jurisdictional authority to investigate 'state' crimes and murder was a state crime. FBI would, ordinarily, never get involved in local murders when state law enforcement was running a case. J. Edgar Hoover and his FBI team needed a strategy (or had to invent one) to take over the investigation in the State of Florida, legitimately.

Once they did take it over, the FBI, at first, seemed reluctant to admit it was a 'racial' killing. Perhaps suggesting other parties could be involved in the murders at the outset would soften the public response to an apparent racial assassination?

Florida's Attorney General, Howard McGrath, was cooperative. Florida could not afford anymore controversy so; he was pleased for the intervention. He made it easier for the entry of the FBI. McGrath alerted the press that the FBI would be given complete cooperation to investigate the assassinations of Harry and Harriette Moore, regardless of traditional jurisdiction issues.

But American anger sprung up across the country while foreign countries watched and expressed their antipathy for this 'terrorist act.' A flurry of telegrams and letters flooded the White House and the Governor's mansion in Florida. United Nations member countries shouted heated accusations of hypocrisy in America, so-called 'land of the free.'

At the UN Assembly, in Paris, William L. Patterson, head of the Civil Rights Congress (CRC), announced his accusation of 'genocide' against America. First there was Groveland and now Harry and Harriette Moore. He was outraged.

An indignant Eleanor Roosevelt rose to object to the 'genocide' accusation. But she did agree that the assassinations of Harry and Harriette Moore were, indeed, a national disgrace. Her objection to the charge of 'genocide' fell on deaf ears.

In truth, for several centuries, America had allowed citizens of color to been lynched, assassinated, murdered, marginalized, disgraced, raped, bombed, brutalized, humiliated, and penalized without regard for human rights, due process, rule of law, civil rights, dignity, justice, liberty, or the American Constitution.

These were facts.

Eleanor Roosevelt could deny the 'genocide' accusation as much as she wanted to, but the truth was not on her side. Racism has resided in the 'fabric' of American society since long before its formation as a country. It was in the DNA.

President Truman feared racial tensions would flare up and turn into race riots if the investigation was not handled effectively. Many cities had suffered through race riots. And riots cost lives, collateral damage, and political capital.

With the assassinations of the Moores, many Americans (both white and black) were enraged that America was unable to protect its citizens, regardless of color, race, nationality, or religion. President Truman realized that at very least, America could show good faith by bringing the perpetrators to justice.

So the FBI developed a plan. Instead of opening 'a murder investigation,' the Bureau opened 'a civil rights investigation.' Civil rights violations fell within their jurisdiction. Once FBI snared perpetrators for civil rights violations, guilty parties might (they hoped) turn on other conspirators who could turn on the actual killers of Harry and Harriette Moore and possibly the Florida Terror bombings, too.

At least this was the theory.

There is also a double-edged sword where FBI investigations are concerned, and particularly so in the South. When the Bureau had jurisdiction in civil rights-related cases, it often could not rely on witness cooperation. White-populated juries will often disregard evidence which FBI would provide, and release guilty parties out of spite. There have been many stunning miscarriages of justice in the South for precisely this reason. And in the 50's it was a given.

A tragic irony of all this is that 'lynching' was not, and is still <u>not,</u> considered a Federal crime. This year Senators Cory Booker, Kamala Harris, and Tim Scott introduced an anti-lynching bill on July 13th, 2018. New York Times reported that: "Nearly 200 anti-lynching bills were introduced in Congress from 1882 to 1986. None were approved. More than 4,000 people were lynched in the United States from 1882 to 1968. The documented killings have been recorded as having occurred in all but four states."

The bombings in 1951 and 52 were the product of 'pattern behavior' (psychologists call it 'anti-social personality disorder') which is generally applied to a criminal individual or group; a term originated by criminal analysts over many years. Even Sir Arthur Conan Doyle's Sherlock Holmes had an apt name for it. He called it "continuity of behavior." But even with established patterns, the FBI could not make a case.

Charles W. Cherry, Sr. *(left)* believed in equal rights for all people, particularly in Daytona Beach and the state of Florida. He was a decorated Korean Conflict veteran and served as a Bethune-Cookman College educator and its business manager, a realtor, a newspaper and radio station owner, and served four terms as a Daytona Beach City Commissioner.

As one of the state's few African-American bail bondsman, he worked to get civil rights protestors, including fellow Morehouse College graduate Dr. Martin Luther King, Jr., released from Florida jails in the 1960s. He was also a former NAACP President and friend of the Moore family.

He had this to say:

"In my own opinion, I don't think it (FBI investigation) was as thorough as it could have been and the reason perhaps was that it allegedly involved some people who were high up in politics and held political offices here in the state of Florida."

The Florida Terror bombings carried a specific message for Floridians of color, of the Jewish faith, and of the Catholic faith. The assassinations of Harry T. and Harriette V. Moore sent one to Floridians of color.

And with both, the messages were the same: "Better behave, or else."

Chapter 8

J. EDGAR HOOVER

W hile FBI involvement in the Moore and Florida Terror cases seemed like a sound decision, FBI Director J. Edgar Hoover and President Harry Truman were acutely aware that Florida's law enforcement and judicial communities were incapable of investigating themselves with any degree of integrity.

Outlandish, racially-tainted, verdicts from all-white juries in Florida confirmed this, with the Groveland case being the most recent event. And with so many Floridians who were members of the KKK (or affiliated with), it was undeniable that Florida law enforcement was ill-equipped and ill-suited to manage any investigation where it had to investigate 'its own'. The Harry T. Moore assassinations, the Groveland Four trials, the Florida Terror bombings, multiple lynchings, and a lengthy history of racial crimes filled the front pages of Florida newspapers on a daily basis.

FBI Forensics Lab

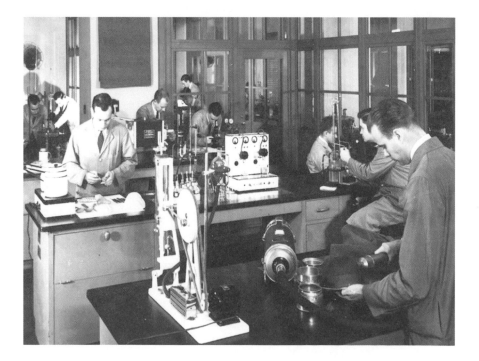

Societal, legal, economic, criminal, and racial conflicts were front and center in the Sunshine State, and the KKK was still bombing Florida, running rampant.

Optics on Florida were abysmal, both nationally and globally. America, the icon of freedom and liberty, the land where 'all men are created equal,' 'land of the free,' was harshly criticized for being absurdly dishonest and hypocritical.

The series of riots which had erupted in cities across the nation was brutal, with massive collateral damage and substantial loss of life. Black war veterans returning home faced gruesome treatment. And the American public grew weary of "lip service" without action. America was at a breaking point. And race crimes were on the increase.

Negative domestic and global opinions of America rang loudly with 'this stench of hypocrisy.' But with the FBI handling the Harry T. Moore assassinations, perhaps some credibility could be earned? The weight of the FBI's investigation would, at least, demonstrate to America and the world, that the assassination of the Moores was not going to be tolerated or ignored. It would be given highest priority by the top law enforcement arm of the government, the FBI, with all of its assets and manpower.

The day after Christmas, in 1951, the FBI launched a comprehensive investigation, dedicating over seventy-eight Special Agents and investigating (or interviewing) nearly one thousand five hundred people in Florida, Alabama, Georgia and North and South Carolina.

The FBI commenced sifting through remains of the Moore home, and elements they gathered were analyzed by FBI's forensic laboratories. They began their search for the killers with interviews and investigative efforts over five states.

To examine the multitude of players in so many locations FBI employed surveillance teams and made use of FBI informants (usually KKK members) across state lines.

J. Edgar Hoover was the only Director the FBI ever had, until his death in May of 1972.

The Rosenbergs

He was first appointed to run what started out as the Bureau of Investigation in the mid-1920's, and by 1935 he was instrumental in establishing the newly formed Federal Bureau of Investigation.

The FBI quickly earned credibility as a federal law enforcement organization. But for all the positives, there were more negatives, where J. Edgar Hoover was concerned. Hoover abused his position over decades with tactics which were often illegal in his effort to ensure his stranglehold on power.

Some say he was a controversial figure. But that is a 'politically polite' term which refers, in this case, to a narcissistic, power-hungry bully. His abuses of power were staggering in scope, and there were so many over many decades. Congressional hearings would later expose his deeds after his death.

The FBI organization became a platform to amplify his own beliefs, fears, ego, and personal attitudes about America. He harassed, threatened, arrested, abused, wire-tapped, profiled, marginalized, slandered, attacked, disgraced and imprisoned many Americans. That he got away with this for so long is a testament to the power of fear.

Congressional hearings finally revealed Hoover's files, instructions, orders, strategies, letters, and communications, which exposed a grotesque array of threatening actions he took against Presidents, Congressmen, political dissenters, Senators, Democrats, liberals, minorities, journalists, musicians, publishers, authors, scientists, gays, activists, foreigners -- and his favorite target: African Americans.

In an article *"Just Being Black Was Enough to Get Yourself Spied on by J. Edgar Hoover's FBI"* published by *The Nation*, January 22, 2014, writer Betty Medsger writes:

"J. Edgar Hoover's FBI spied on people in many political movements — the antiwar movement, the civil rights movement, the women's movement, the gay rights movement, the environmental movement. They also were harassed, sometimes violently." Documents were published after his passing which revealed many prejudiced beliefs and alarming attitudes. One such observation indicates that to Hoover: "Blacks were the same as Communists."

Until unknown people burglarized the FBI office in Media, Pennsylvania, the night of March 8, 1971, there was only suspicion, not evidence, that the FBI actively worked to suppress dissent. When some of those burglars stepped forward and identified themselves for the first time, they were widely praised for exposing Hoover's secret FBI, a step that ignited the first national debate on the role of intelligence agencies in a democratic society and, along with other developments, led, by 1975, to the first congressional investigations of all intelligence agencies and bureau reforms.

Searching for evidence of whether dissent was being suppressed was William Davidon's goal. Given the lack of any official oversight of intelligence agencies, the Haverford College physics professor thought burglary would be the only way to get documentary evidence of whether the FBI was repressing activists. Under his leadership, the eight-member Citizens Commission to Investigate the FBI, the name the burglars gave themselves, found and gave the public much evidence that such suppression was taking place.

One of the Media files was a policy statement so brazen that, as some editorial writers stated at the time, it seemed more like what might be found in the files of the Soviet KGB or the East German Stasi rather than in the files of an intelligence or law enforcement agency in a democratic society. In it, FBI agents were urged to "enhance the paranoia......get the point across there is an FBI agent behind every mailbox."

The files revealed that even people who expressed mild liberal opposition to the war or support for civil rights in letters to newspaper editors or in correspondence to their congressional representative acquired dossiers, were added to FBI files. Most of these targets came to the FBI's attention because of ideas they expressed, or ideas informers surmised they held.

But the Media files revealed that African-Americans, Hoover's largest targeted group, didn't have to be perceived as having liberal, or even radical or subversive, ideas to merit being spied on. Nor was it necessary for them to engage in violent behavior to become a watched person. Being black was enough.

The Media files revealed directives that required FBI field offices to watch African-Americans wherever they went—in churches, in classrooms, on college campuses, in bars, in restaurants, in bookstores, in their places of employment, in stores, in any social setting, in their neighborhoods and even at the front doors of their homes. Probably few of them realized that the bill collector at their door might be an FBI informer.

In an analysis of the Media files in summer 1971, then–Washington Post reporter William Greider wrote that the files offered "the public and Congress an unprecedented glimpse of how the U.S. government watches its citizens—particularly black citizens."

It conducted such spying, he wrote, in ways that were as unreasonable as it would have been for the bureau to have spied on all lawyers who engaged in politics because, "as everyone knows, some lawyers in politics turn out to be crooks."

Consider the requirements discovered in the Media files: every agent had to have at least one informer who reported to him regularly on the activities of black people. In Washington, DC, every agent was required to assign six informers to spy on black people. This requirement was so important in the bureau that exemption from it was an elaborate bureaucratic process. Agents in an FBI office in a community where no black people lived were required to "specify by memorandum form 170-6 with a copy for the RA (Resident Agency, what small FBI offices like Media were called) error folder so that he will not be charged with failure to perform."

An assignment to build a large network of informers throughout the black neighborhoods of Philadelphia included these recommendations on who should be recruited: men honorably discharged from the armed services and members of veterans organizations; friends, relatives and acquaintances of bureau employees; "employees and owners of businesses in ghetto areas which might include taverns, liquor stores, drug stores, pawn shops, gunships, barber shops, janitors of apartment buildings, etc."

Bureau officials also suggested that agents establish contact with "persons who frequent ghetto areas on a regular basis such as taxi drivers, salesmen, distributors of newspapers, food, and beverages. Installment collectors might also be considered in this regard."

In other words, at that time, anybody a black person encountered might have been an FBI informer. The agent in charge of the Philadelphia office wrote in a memorandum that some restaurants and lounges were places where "militant Negroes were known to congregate."

As Greider noted, the Media files prescribing racial surveillance "sound like instructions for agents being sent to a foreign country."

The director regarded the need for black informers on campuses as urgent. He required agents to investigate and infiltrate every black student organization at two-year colleges as well as four-year colleges and universities, and to do so without regard for whether there had been disturbances on those campuses. "We must develop a network of discreet quality sources in a position to furnish required information," he wrote.

All black students at Swarthmore College were under surveillance. The Black Student Union at Pennsylvania Military College in Chester, Pennsylvania, was described in a file as peaceful and loosely knit, a "basically dormant" group. Nevertheless, the bureau concluded it would "open cases" on the leaders of this group that had "possibly as few as a half dozen" members.

When the nature of COINTELPRO—counterintelligence programs Hoover operated since 1956—was revealed in December 1973 on orders of a judge in a lawsuit brought by NBC journalist Carl Stern, the public learned that efforts in these programs to destroy individuals and organizations ranged from crude to cruel.

Antiwar activists' oranges were injected with powerful laxatives. Prostitutes known to have STDs were hired in an effort to entrap leaders of the Fair Play for Cuba Committee.

But in these, the most vicious of Hoover's operations, the worst operations seem to have been reserved for black people. For example, a bureau informer provided an apartment diagram that guided a Chicago police shooter to "Fred's bed" to kill Black Panther Fred Hampton as he slept. In internal documents, the FBI proudly took credit for the killing of Hampton and Mark Clark, another Black Panther, that night. The informer was given a bonus for his role in what the bureau called a successful raid.

False testimony by an FBI informer sent Geronimo Pratt, a Los Angeles Black Panther, to prison for twenty-seven years for a murder conviction that was overturned in 1997 by a judge who ruled the bureau had concealed evidence that would have acquitted Pratt.

Surely the most egregious among all the Hoover political operations were the ones conducted against the Reverend Dr. Martin Luther King Jr. Top FBI officials sat in their offices a few blocks from where King delivered his "I Have a Dream" speech at the 1963 March on Washington, listening to the speech on radios. As 250,000 people on the Washington Mall cherished King's call for racial justice and racial harmony, FBI officials decided it was the speech of a demagogue who should be toppled by the bureau.

The following year, just days before he was to receive the Nobel Peace Prize, the bureau sent him tapes intended as blackmail to convince him to commit suicide.

When the head of the bureau's Racial Intelligence Section, George Moore, testified before the Church Committee, the Senate committee that investigated all intelligence committees in 1975, he was asked if, during the execution of COINTELPRO operations, anybody at the FBI had discussed the operations' constitutionality or legality. He responded: "No, we never gave it a thought."

Revelations about the blanket surveillance and extreme treatment of African-Americans by the FBI suggest that African-Americans' efforts to claim their most basic rights as citizens may have been delayed for decades, in part, by an FBI director who cautioned presidents against supporting their efforts. Their demands for equality, he said, were inspired by communists and, as such, should be ignored.

These injustices against black people and ones against countless other Americans came to light only because eight people, who seemed as ordinary as most next-door neighbors, found extraordinary courage and, willing to risk spending many years in prison, stole FBI files in 1971 that revealed this scandalous situation that had by then existed near the top of the federal government for nearly a half-century."

J. Edgar Hoover was one of the most powerful men in America. But that power was grotesquely abused through his willingness to blackmail and threaten anyone to maintain his power.

It is likely he may have done his most significant damage not through action, but through his inaction in refusing to protect the fundamental human rights of black citizens. Tens of thousands of human lives were damaged or destroyed by actions, direct and indirect, by omission.

At every stage in his life and career, Hoover diligently toiled to undermine black progress. He despised African Americans as much as communists and conflated the two, seeking to prove that the civil rights movement was 'a communist plot.' And his treatment of the media who dared to expose his misdeeds were harassed mercilessly."

U.S. President Harry Truman lamented that Hoover had transformed the FBI into his own private secret police force.

Said President Truman of Hoover...

"...we want no Gestapo or secret police. The FBI is tending in that direction. They are dabbling in sex-life scandals and plain blackmail. J. Edgar Hoover would give his right eye to take over, and all congressmen and senators are afraid of him."

J. Edgar Hoover personally supervised the Harry T. Moore assassination investigation.

Chapter 9

THE RED SCARE

W hen investigations are launched, it is crucial to understand the context of the crime, before, during, and after the event. Crimes rarely occur in a 'bubble'. And many factors will impact a case, sending investigators in directions they could never have imagined.

In the cases of the Harry T. Moore and the Florida Terror bombings, what happened at the outset was peculiar.

Florida newspapers, en masse, intimated that responsibility for the bombings in Florida likely lay at the feet of 'communist infiltrators' allegedly seeking to cause a race war between blacks and whites in America. Many politicians and company owners swore that 'their blacks were happy' and that these commu-

nists were troublemakers trying to disrupt law-biding American society. The word 'troublemaker' was popular in the South.

Surprisingly, the FBI concurred, about the potentiality of Communists bombing Florida, at least in the beginning. Most newspapers pointed to Communist conspiracies in play, allegedly attempting to trigger America's downfall. Of course, there was no evidence to justify such comments.

Remarkably, politicians, company owners, journalists, investigators, police officers, and public figures all concurred with the conspiracy theory early on in the investigation. It appeared to be convenient and diverted blame away from Florida's citizenry and the state.

While the crimes in Florida were racially-motivated, the idea that communists might somehow be involved, added one more layer of enthusiastic motivation for Hoover to personally supervise the investigation of the Moore assassinations. After all, if the 'communist' theory was correct, it could have been a big win for communist conspiracy devotees. And J. Edgar Hoover was at the head of the pack where this was concerned.

These influences are mentioned with purpose. If during the Harry T. Moore bombing investigation there was a generally accepted predisposition to focus attention in alternate directions, rather than to obvious criminal candidates, investigators could easily have been distracted, then diverted by random conspiracy theories; potentially allowing real perpetrators to evade capture.

Every law enforcement officer knows the first hours after any crime is committed are crucial and generally yield the best evidence during an investigation.

Russia's first atomic bomb RDS-1

To make my point, an FBI spokesman was interviewed in the press early on in the Moore investigation where he indicated they were investigating the possible motives of NAACP members, family members, and possible black suspects in the community. High on the FBI menu of suspects were potential communist agitators.

In this era, this was what they called 'The 'Red Scare.'

The Red Scare had taken hold and become hyperactive in American society. The scare spread via gossip, radio, newspapers, television (wherever it could broadcast), law enforcement, misinformation, manipulation, ignorance, and public fear.

The relationship between Soviet Russia and America had become strained after the end of World War ll. Then in 1949, the Soviet Union tested its first nuclear weapon, much to the dismay of America.

However, the Russians had been developing atomic power since 1938. Soviets feared German aggression just before World War Two started, so Stalin was hoping to see his country develop some form of 'super weapon' to halt any future invasion by Germany, should it become necessary.

But World War Two was over before Russia mastered the technology to detonate their nuclear bomb. The bomb they finally did develop was called RDS-1. It's detonation sent an electric shock through the American public and its military.

Concurrently, Indochina was awash with Viet Minh soldiers engaging French occupiers in Viet Nam. Adding fuel to the fire, the Viet Minh had gained support from Communist China and the Soviet Union.

Then North Korea invaded South Korea in June of 1950, once again backed by Communist China and Soviet Russia. It was clear that Russia was no ally to America anymore; China never was. The Cold War was on and, Communism appeared to be advancing across the globe.

To make matters more suspicious and compelling, in March of 1951, Julius and Ethel Rosenberg were found guilty of espionage, for allegedly passing atomic secrets to the Soviets.

Attorney Roy Cohn and Senator Joseph McCarthy

Fear grew in the hearts and minds of Americans and motivated fear-mongering, self-serving opportunist, Senator Joe McCarthy, to launch a 'shock and awe' mud-slinging campaign pointing fingers at alleged 'American Communist conspirators'.

McCarthy (with the support of J. Edgar Hoover) had many Americans convinced (or fearful) that communist infiltrators were going to bring down America. He also managed to convince Americans that he was the country's 'white knight' ready to find these evil perpetrators and save democracy. He sold this as 'noble.' The truth was otherwise.

McCarthy became the 'poster boy' for a ruthless crusade against alleged communists in America, mostly without reason or evidence. Not one Soviet spy was ever caught during McCarthy's savage, nationally-damaging witch hunt.

McCarthy could not (or did not want to) differentiate between being a communist and being a spy. Or if ever he could, it didn't seem to matter. It became an egocentric feeding frenzy which the press ate up.

McCarthy sold newspapers on a grand scale and the hearings received unprecedented national coverage. The rage and fever for good ratings, good earnings, fueled by unprecedented hysteria ruled the moment and the bank accounts. And McCarthy got the attention he so desperately craved.

For a time, McCarthy was a 'master manipulator' of the media, as were Hitler and Mussolini and so many others; but eventually, America saw through him and he was marginalized, then ousted, thankfully. The American public and its government were unduly influenced by the hypocrisy of his actions and were tainted with national disgrace by what he had become.

Internationally, America was criticized for condoning his pathological behavior. His 'reign of fear' triggered a tsunami of human damage; his legacy was the proof to America that fear is all you need to gain power. Fear is a 'bond that ties.'

Figures such as McCarthy and Hoover fanned the flames of fear by wildly exaggerating that possibility. As the Red Scare intensified, the political climate turned increasingly conservative. Elected officials from both major parties sought to portray themselves as staunch anticommunists, and few people dared to criticize the questionable tactics used to persecute suspected radicals.

Mussolini and Hitler

Mao Tse Tung and Joseph Stalin

Membership in leftist groups dropped as it became clear that such associations could lead to severe consequences, and dissenting voices from the left side of the political spectrum fell silent on a range of important issues. In judicial affairs, for example, support for free speech and other civil liberties eroded significantly.

Americans also felt the effects of the Red Scare on a personal level as thousands of alleged communist sympathizers saw their lives disrupted. They were harassed by law enforcement, alienated from friends and family, and fired from their jobs.

While a small number of the accused may have been aspiring revolutionaries, most others were the victims of false allegations or had done nothing more than exercising their democratic right to join a political party.

Though the climate of fear and repression began to ease in the late 1950s, the Red Scare has continued to influence political debate in the decades since and is often cited as an example of how unfounded fears can compromise civil liberties.

The 1950's was a fierce era, subjugated by threats, manipulations, nationalism, racism, political ambitions, abuse of power, peonage, wars, ignorance, violence, and fear, perpetuated and magnified by chaos and greed.

Senator McCarthy's methods were manipulative and particularly effective with his ability to manipulate the press and the media, in general. Create a common enemy and bind everyone to the cause of the enemy's destruction, with 'fear' being the operative word.

Manipulation is a favorite element and a common strategy used by politicians but particularly popular, in the extreme, with dictators: Joseph Stalin, Adolf Hitler, Benito Mussolini, Pol Pot, Idi Amin Dada, Vladimir Lenin, Mao Tse Tung, all of them.

Fear, in the wrong hands, readily influences a populace who are easily frightened and then intimidated into handing over political power.

Those who desire this power for egocentric or pathological reasons have used these tactics for centuries, always to the detriment of those whom they ruled. Adolf Hitler took precisely this same path in pre-war Germany to take control.

He made false economic promises, used chaos, fear, and threats, then manipulation to create a common enemy (the Jews), which allowed him to take control, become a dictator and go to war. This method is common. The public appears to fall for these falsehoods (false promises and personality cults) far too easily, partly out of delusion, wishful thinking, desperation, and always fear. Anyone lusting for power uses this operating method.

Many powerful fascists preceded Senator McCarthy's small 'blip on the radar,' and so many have come after, who were more prominent and more terrifying.

But in 1950's America, if one needed to blame something or someone for any reason, whether they were too liberal, too socialist, too progressive, too union-minded, too left, too different, or just not American enough, they merely shouted the word 'communist.' The damage done by McCarthy can still be felt today.

Fear of communism infected America's government and law enforcement like a pandemic, which is, in part, why the Ku Klux Klan was not immediately named as a likely perpetrator of race crimes committed in Florida. The Red Scare had become palpable; national hysteria had officially taken hold; everything bad had to be 'communist.'

These circumstances created an ideal ('perfect storm') moment to blame fictitious third parties, insurgents, rival politicians, communists, journalists, blacks, and liberals, while hoping to take control of America at any cost.

Chapter 10

WORLD WAR II

"We were at war, and in war, you don't have friendly relationships, you're out to kill each other. That's how it was at the Courier (newspaper). We were trying to kill Jim Crow and racism. They didn't seem to understand that we had every right to fight for full citizenship at home if we were expected to give our lives overseas."

~ Edna Chappelle McKenzie, Journalist/Historian

America's entering World War ll against Nazi Germany created an opportunity for civil rights activism to gain significant traction.

The mood in America was changing rapidly. And with it came a very unexpected opportunity. African Americans who 'signed up' to enter the military had a chance to escape the drudgery of unemployment and racism in America, go to a foreign country with pay, and prove their worth in a unique way for their country.

Adolf Hitler's racist rhetoric was explicit. And most countries around the world condemned Germany's virulent racism. The liberal and black press in America joined the fray to condemn such racism but compared it to the exploits of Jim Crow America. While Nazi Germany looked evil for its racist antics, America would fall under the watchful eyes of the world, by comparison.

Few of us today can begin to understand what a World War feels like or how it impacts the psyche of the entire world. Everything changed. No country on the planet escaped the savage impact of the fight between fascism and freedom.

And while racial injustices were ever present in America, many blacks hoped for a better situation upon joining the army to fight for freedom. However, Jim Crow-style segregation was virulent in the American military too. During the war, many blacks, once again, suffered humiliation, segregation, violence, injustice, and overall extreme racism before, during, and after combat.

Black troops were always segregated during basic training. In battle, blacks fought beside blacks only, and it was a rare moment where blacks and whites went into action side-by-side.

All black regiments were under the command of white officers. And white soldiers very often mistreated black soldiers, in many cases, brutally. Racial confrontations on military bases caused violent clashes, and in some cases, full-on race riots.

Before going into combat, soldiers were required to donate blood so there would be an adequate blood reserve in readiness for the war wounded. However, black blood supplies were kept separately from white blood storage, always. This did not go unnoticed by blacks. Just another slight for them to process.

The military establishment worked hard to keep racial discord quiet, but the black press often got wind of the stories and published regardless, fur-

Corporal William E. Thomas and Private First Class Joseph Jackson on Easter Morning, March 10, 1945.

ther deepening the government's mistrust of the media, motivating J. Edgar Hoover to threaten and harass the press on a national scale.

After the dust of war settled in America, the country was in a profound state of shock.

There remained deep-rooted fears, broken alliances, international mistrust, post-traumatic stress disorder on a monumental scale, extreme polarization, economic hardship, national anxieties, racial tensions, and pervasive distrust.

Add to that, the many Americans who suffered staggering personal losses of loved ones during the global conflict.

World War II changed America. And the comparisons between white supremacy and Hitler's "master race" were inevitable. Jim Crow behaviors

shocked many of the United Nations delegates who reported home about the American practice of segregating blacks.

During the war, many black Americans had the opportunity to experience other societies, peoples, and cultures, and they saw first-hand how fascism made a crude attempt to dismember freedom and erase liberty. But upon returning to America, Jim Crow was waiting for them.

African American soldiers returned from the war with a priority commitment to fight for equality and dignity on American soil.

Whether it was economic, political, racial, historical, or cultural - everything was in flux. And so was society. The polarization in America was extreme between right and left. The Supreme Court, Department of Justice, law enforcement, Congress, the press, all the trappings that go with these, were splintering quietly, and in some cases erupting loudly.

J. Edgar Hoover championed (throughout his life) a peacetime Anti-Sedition Act in America. He wanted to contain (or crush) liberals, blacks, minorities, gays, and anyone who was too liberal-leaning. Black publishers were clear-headed about the state of America and how it needed to change, but Hoover's FBI made 'a run' at all of them.

Edna Chappelle McKenzie was an award-winning journalist, and the first black woman to earn a doctorate at the University of Pittsburgh. She launched her writing career at the Courier Newspaper as a society reporter in the 1940s. She quickly moved to the news desk and covered hard news alongside the men.

Armed with her favorite phrase "tell the truth," Edna was particularly focused on documenting black history. She believed history should be used to empower, inform and teach, and that blacks should never be ashamed of their history. "Edna was fearless," said her closest friend. "She always said, 'I just want to tell the truth, to write the truth.' That if this country knew the truth about black history, it would change things."

Edna Chappelle McKenzie

In 1942, a news war campaign called "Double Victory" was launched by the Courier Newspaper. It became a rallying cry for black journalists, activists and citizens to secure both victories over *fascism* abroad during World War II and victory over *racism* at home.

As of this writing, the latest Federal Anti-Lynching Bill introduced to Congress is a yet another indicator of the unfortunate rift dividing America, where human values, respect, justice, and dignity are concerned. That Southern states (and others) resisted support of this in over 200 attempts, is astonishing. While the Double Victory campaign began during the World War II era, it has still not seen victory 75 years later.

"There is a historical relationship between Nazism and white supremacy in the United States. But collective amnesia had consequences. When Americans celebrated the country's victory in World War II, many black veterans returned to America only to be denied jobs or housing; it became all the more difficult to talk honestly about racism today."

Winning World War ll was only a partial victory with black soldiers returning home to face more racial discrimination.

Beginning in 1943, race riots erupted across the country. Over two hundred interracial incidents were documented in cities and military bases across America. Civil unrest was amplified by a war fought on other continents that caused returning veterans to expect the freedom for which they fought and died to be afforded them at home.

Advocates of the Double Victory campaign understood that Nazism would not be wholly vanquished until white supremacy was defeated in America.

*The Parks &
Recreation Team
who Shares Daily
the Legacy of
the Moores.*

*Top row (l-r) Mr. Jeff Davis, North Area Parks Operations Manager
& Mrs. Sonya Mallard, Cultural Center Coordinator.
Bottom row (l-r) Mr. Dustin Moore, Cultural Center Aide &
Mrs. Carshonda Wright, Cultural Center Leader*

*Top row (l-r) Mr. William Gary, President, Harry T. &
Harriette V. Moore Cultural Complex, Inc. & Mr. Art Edward, Board Member
Bottom row (l-r) Mrs. Joyce Aron, Mrs. Cindy Flachmeier, Mrs. Lucy Seigler,
Board Members of the Harry T. & Harriette V. Moore Cultural Complex, Inc.*

Top Back Row (l-r) Mr. Theodis Ray, Mr. Leroy Smith, Mr. James Fletcher
Bottom Row (l r) Mrs. Jessie Robinson, Mrs. Gloria Bartley, Mrs. Reva Watson,
Mrs. Charlie Smith, Mrs. Elouise Boatwright

The Home-Going Services for Mrs. Juanita Evangeline Moore was held at Shiloh African Methodist Episcopal Church in Mims, Florida, Pastor Joyce Harvey presiding.

The horse-drawn carriage procession taking Mrs. Juanita Evangeline Moore to her final resting place going through the Harry T. & Harriette V. Moore Memorial Park & Museum to LaGrange Cemetery in Mims, Florida.

Gravesites of Harry, Harriette and Juanita Evangeline Moore.

Replica of the Moores' Home

Original oil on wood painting by distinguished award winning
South Florida Artist Peter Olsen

(l-r) Mr. William Gary, President and Mr. Walter T. Shaw, Producer, Top Cat II Production Publishing Group

Bishop Jimmie Williams Pastor of Lighthouse Worship Center

"Greater love hath no man than this, that a man lay down his life for his friends."

John 15:13 KJV

Chapter 11
BEAUTIFUL FLORIDA

Before the deaths of the Moores yet another set of circumstances was in play. Another mindset impacted the nation. And it created a layer of expectations in American society.

Florida, after World War ll, was attempting to offer the bright Florida image of a user-friendly, progressive, family environment, with business opportunities aplenty.

Every state put their best foot forward to create an appealing image for its growth and bright future, however, in Florida's case, with horrific 'race crimes' in progress over a lengthy period, its public image could be savaged if the Florida Terror bombings continued. And the Groveland Case was a problem.

At the end of World War ll, America was back in business, or that was the hope. Nearly two million residents of Florida had gone to war and, now they were coming home. It was what they called "the postwar boom."

Amusingly, immediately following Japan's surrender, pollster George Gallop asked Americans to which state they would most like to move. California and Florida ranked first and second.

"The Florida Dream" swelled during this era. Florida was the cheaper alternative to California. Buoyed by prosperity and the lure of romantic beaches with a warm climate.

Soon migrants began to pour into the Sunshine State. Florida's population grew from 1.9 million residents in 1940 to 2.7 million inhabitants a decade later.

And by 1950, residents of Miami and Jacksonville watched the first television signals beamed in Florida. While, annually, hundreds of thousands of visitors enjoyed tourist attractions such as Cypress Gardens, Marineland, and Silver Springs.

Somehow bombings became the new priority over building the economy where the Klan was concerned. They did not want to see Jews, Catholics, and more blacks invading their neighborhoods. Florida's economy needed a boost to continue to rebuild, to develop, to attract new business and meaningful investment. The last thing the State wanted was a reputation for serial bombings, assassinations, murders, Ku Klux Klan parades, and race crimes. Yet all of these incidents were active in Florida.

If Florida had to admit to Ku Klux Klan responsibility for these local crimes it would signify that the state had taken 'ownership' of the bombings. It

was healthier to nominate a rogue outsider (communist infiltrators) than to take responsibility for these horrific events currently under investigation in Florida.

In looking at the context of America and Florida at this time in history, it's certainly understandable how historical events had been manipulated and 'white-washed' solely for the purpose of inventing a more palatable view of the state.

But in due time, well above the horizon for *all* to see, a dark cloud hovered over Florida. Its name was Jim Crow.

JIM CROW

The origin of the name "Jim Crow" is derived from the phrase "Jump Jim Crow," a demeaning song-and-dance caricature of blacks performed by a white actor named Thomas Rice who did it in blackface. He first performed for audiences in 1832.

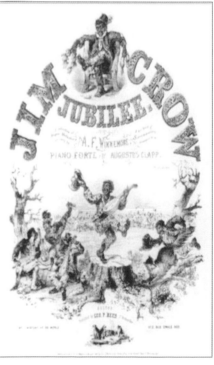

Jim Crow laws were state and local laws which enforced racial segregation primarily in the Southern United States. As a result of Rice's fame, "Jim Crow" by 1838 had become a racist expression meaning "Negro." When southern legislatures passed laws of racial segregation directed against blacks at the end of the 19th century, these statutes became known as 'Jim Crow laws.'

Enacted by white-dominated state legislatures in the late 19th century after the Reconstruction period, these laws continued to be enforced as recently as 1965.

These laws mandated racial segregation in all public facilities in the states of the former Confederate States of America, starting in the 1870s and 1880s, and upheld by the United States Supreme Court's Plessy vs. Ferguson Supreme Court Decision "separate but equal" doctrine aimed at African Americans.

Public education had been segregated since its establishment in most of the South after the Civil War.

The idea was extended to public facilities and transportation, including segregated cars on interstate trains and, later, buses. Facilities for African Americans were consistently inferior and underfunded compared to those which were then available to whites; and often they did not exist at all.

This hateful law endorsed and institutionalized extreme economic, social, and educational disadvantages and deprived African Americans of the most basic human needs and entitlements. The comparisons to South Africa's infamous Apartheid Laws are frighteningly similar. This was, after all, "American Apartheid".

Segregation was vigorously and violently enforced in Southern states, while Northern segregation often played out in different ways. It was implemented, for the most part, via ghetto creation, housing segregation, bank lending practices, and job discrimination.

The U.S. military was segregated, regardless of any southern enforcements. President Woodrow Wilson, also a Southerner, initiated highly restrictive segregation of federal workplaces at the request of Southern Cabinet members as early as 1913.

Other restrictions against blacks dated back to 1865 when their civil rights and civil liberties were also congressionally restricted. And dozens more restrictions were imposed by Congress and the Supreme Court over the next century.

In fact, restriction of civil rights and civil liberties for African Americans had been a fact for nearly two centuries before America was even a country.

The centuries of abuse they endured living under American democracy was horrific.

Chapter 12

SIX MONTHS
AFTER THE BOMBING

The investigation of the Moore assassinations continued. By mid-1952, six months after the killings of the Moores, no arrests had been made. Many Americans began to fret. The FBI had not yet harnessed their resources nor thoroughly analyzed the available evidence sufficiently to issue indictments of persons of interest.

The trail grew colder with each passing month. The NAACP stated that Americans were becoming disappointed in their government and the FBI. With dozens of suspects and persons of interest, there seemed to be no progress.

After three years without any indictments and no suspects 'on deck.' A disappointed public began to view the FBI investigation as a failure. Some accused the government of not making a legitimate effort. Some called it a 'show without substance'; some called it 'a sham.'

Stetson Kennedy

And some, like the author, activist, journalist Stetson Kennedy suspected 'corruption' at the FBI.

Stetson was a highly-regarded author, journalist, folklorist, and human rights activist. He worked with author and journalist, Zora Neale Hurston and renowned folklorist, Alan Lomax. But he also worked for the Georgia Bureau of Investigation where he went undercover to expose the Ku Klux Klan.

He authored such books as "The Klan Unmasked," "Jim Crow Guide to the U.S.A., "The Florida Slave," and more. Kennedy had reason to attack the FBI.

Kennedy met with Jefferson (J.J.) Elliott, Governor Fuller Warren's Special Investigator. On a hunch, and because Kennedy had experience dealing with Klan members, he offhandedly offered a verbally coded sign to Elliott. The Klan uses a coded message to identify each other, to be sure.

To Kennedy's shock and dismay, Elliott responded with the authentic, active Ku Klux Klan response.

A surprised Stetson Kennedy immediately flew to Washington to inform the FBI that Governor Fuller Warren's Special Investigator in current civil rights crimes (including, but not only, the Groveland Four and Harry T. Moore cases) was an active member of the Ku Klux Klan.

Kennedy reported it (plus additional information) to the FBI but, they did not respond to, what he assumed would be, game-changing information. After delivering his report, the FBI sidelined him and indicated they were unhappy with his performance.

Later, when there were no FBI indictments handed down on the Harry T. Moore or the Florida Terror bombings, he surmised that the FBI was either complicit in certain racially-motivated crimes, aided suspects who did the Klan's bidding, or that they were not legitimately seeking justice for racial-motivated crimes.

Stetson Kennedy lost faith in the FBI.

On March 7, 1952, the FBI contacted Governor Fuller Warren's office and spoke to Investigator Jeffrey Elliott to determine if the Governor's office had initiated an investigation into the Harry T. Moore case. They had not. Three months had passed and the Governor had done nothing. Later, Elliott would eventually be assigned to the Moore case by Governor Fuller Warren.

Accusations were also made that Elliott was a Klansman. Both Elliott and Governor Warren denied this. However, it was proved to be true.

Elliott later admitted that he had lied and that he really was a Klansman. His position working for the Governor was no secret, therefore, his explanation that it was 'part of his job' to be in the Klan was, of course, absurd. After Elliott's death, his daughter, Violette, was asked if she thought her father had been a Klansman and she replied: "Yes, I believe he was."

Jefferson Elliott's younger daughter, Nelle, stated: "To be truthful, I think all Southerners had a certain amount of bigotry to them."

Those who were concerned about civil and human rights concluded the FBI investigations into the Harry T. Moore and Florida Terror bombings were political posturings, and not functioning with the purpose of exacting justice on behalf of minorities who were its victims.

Meanwhile, J. Edgar Hoover continued with his communist-hunting obsessions. His current target now was scientist, Albert Einstein; his next target would be Martin Luther King.

And racially-motivated crimes continued.

Once the FBI failed to provide a resolution to the Harry T. Moore assassination, the international community heightened its political bashing of America for the false image and misrepresentations of its 'liberty, justice, and freedom for all' slogans. America had many excellent attributes, but America, 'land of the free' was not one of them.

Not long after Hitler rose to power in 1933, world-renowned Albert Einstein (a German Jew) decided never to return to his home in Germany once Hitler's National Socialists took over. Einstein secured a position at the Institute for Advanced Study at Princeton, in New Jersey.

He settled in America in 1940. Upon arriving in America he became critical of what he viewed as 'pre-fascist' behavior where civil rights and liberties were concerned. He saw the signs that America had many societal and political similarities to pre-war Germany under Adolf Hitler.

Having observed pre-war German politics, first-hand, he was particularly aware of the abuses and human rights issues instigated by Adolf Hitler. Einstein spoke plainly about his concerns. Fascism grows and steals power in increments, he stated. Denying minorities civil rights in society was how it started in Berlin.

With his stunning scientific notoriety, he was immediately 'a darling' of the press. His favorite topics were peace, human rights, science, and racism. And he spoke out against racism in both Europe and America.

In 1946, Lincoln University offered him an honorary degree. It happens that Lincoln U. was the first degree-granting college for African-Americans

at that time and it happened to be the alma mater of the late Harry T. Moore's close friend and confidante, Thurgood Marshall, and literary giant, Langston Hughes.

That year Einstein gave a lecture at the university and near its conclusion offered his view on racism in America to the class. He stated that he "did not intend to be quiet" (about his objections to American racism.)

In Einstein's lecture he offered this comment:

"Racism is a disease of white people."

⌒ Albert Einstein

Chapter 13

J. EDGAR HOOVER AGAIN

Because Einstein was a 'foreigner' and a 'liberal,' J. Edgar Hoover became suspicious. Einstein's outspoken anti-racist comments immediately made him a 'suspect.' Hoover was convinced that Einstein had to be a communist. Hoover threw that label at everyone who did not 'fit his point of view.'

With Hoover having his obsession, anyone who criticized America for its civil rights demeanor was more than likely a Marxist, in his view; certainly not a candidate to be a good American.

At his instruction, the FBI immediately began what would become a two-decade-long, comprehensive, illegal, surveillance campaign of Albert Einstein.

Under orders of the 'rabid' anti-communist, Hoover, Special Agents wire-tapped Einstein's phone calls, opened his mail, and studied contents of his garbage cans for decades hoping to expose Einstein as a communist, or even better, a Russian spy. There was no oversight on Hoover. He could harass, investigate, wire-tap, or threaten anyone he wanted at any time.

Twenty-two years of surveillance later, the FBI had accumulated an astounding file on Albert Einstein, at nearly two thousand pages. But there was no communism - no spying - no Marxism. Hoover employed this depth of surveillance on many Americans at his own discretion.

He was as fearful of communists and socialist causes as any paranoid American could be. And he was not shy to support methods of people like Senator Joe McCarthy.

The difference was, Hoover had lifetime powers to invade, obstruct, intimidate, harass, or otherwise ruin American lives, while Senator McCarthy's power burned out in only a few years.

The discussion of 'fear' and 'communism' is not a diversion in exploring the Harry T. Moore bombing. It is pertinent to the analysis of racism and the

FBI Chief Calls Martin Luther King 'The Most Notorious Liar in Country'

By United Press International

WASHINGTON.

FBI director J. Edgar Hoover said yesterday that the Rev. Dr. Martin Luther King Jr. was "the most notorious liar in the country" for claiming FBI agents in Albany, Ga., would take no action on civil rights complaints because they are Southerners.

Caryl Rivers, Washington correspondent of the San Juan, Puerto Rico, newspaper El Mundo, reported that Mr. Hoover made the statement in a group interview with 20 women reporters who arranged periodic meetings with Washington officials.

J. Edgar Hoover

Dr. Martin Luther King

United Press International

investigations into the Moore and the Florida Terror bombings. Conservative paranoia and rampant abuses of power infected all levels of society and government.

And it most certainly affected the operating methods of law enforcement and the American justice system. With J. Edgar Hoover leading the investigation into a civil rights crime, one can only wonder as to the veracity of the methods he used, the investigative process, the intentions, and the final results.

Harry Moore cared only about human rights. But Hoover and men in influential positions wanted to discredit Moore and all who shared in his human rights values. It was too easy to slap a 'communist' label on anyone who was liberal or a minority or a foreigner or black. Hoover, it's been proven, had a pattern of behavior which was flawed and criminal.

Ultra-conservative persons in power selectively chose what suited their belief system and ignored all else in favor of the idea that if you are white, then you are entitled and superior. If ever an ideology resembled South Africa's Apartheid this was it.

Not long after the deaths of the Moores and the passing of Albert Einstein, Hoover shifted his paranoia and energies to Martin Luther King, and other black community leaders, in precisely the same way he had haunted Albert Einstein's life.

By the 1960's, the animosity between Martin Luther King and J. Edgar Hoover was surreal and dangerous.

King denounced the FBI as being "completely ineffectual in resolving the continued mayhem and brutality inflicted upon the Negro in the Deep South." And J. Edgar Hoover responded that King was the "most notorious liar in the country." Hoover's paranoia knew no bounds; neither did his abuses. Yet Martin Luther King was correct in his assessment of the FBI being ineffectual in the South at that time.

Michael E. Ruane/Retropolis
The Washington Post, December 13, 2017

"YOU ARE DONE: A SECRET LETTER TO MARTIN LUTHER KING JR. SHEDS LIGHT ON FBI'S MALICE"

"FBI documents reveal more about the government's preoccupation with the Communist Party in America and J. Edgar Hoover's obsessive hatred for King than it reveals about Martin Luther King personally. The Communist Party by the 1960's had already collapsed into a minor organization with little importance.

"I think the number one takeaway historically is how, even in March of 1968, the FBI continues to be bizarrely preoccupied with how important the Communist Party USA is. ... The Communist Party, by 1968, is of no importance to anything,"

"These incredibly exaggerated statements of communist influence are exactly what the FBI (Hoover) wants to hear." The efforts to pin King as a communist came at a time when the country was still reeling from fears of communist subversion, which had reached a fever pitch when Sen. Joseph McCarthy rose to national prominence in the 1950s with his probes to expose alleged infiltration in the federal government.

This secret letter *(shown on opposite page)* was tucked inside the pages of an old book. It had been written by FBI Director J. Edgar Hoover to a

JOHN EDGAR HOOVER
DIRECTOR

Federal Bureau of Investigation
United States Department of Justice
Washington, D. C.

November 19, 1964

PERSONAL

Dear Bill:

I want to tell you how much I appreciate your note of today concerning the press conference which I had yesterday with the Washington women reporters. I have always been reluctant about holding press conferences and have only held one or two in the period during which I have been Director. However, these women reporters have been most persistent to have a briefing on the work of the Bureau and there were a number of things that I wanted to also get off my chest at the same time, so I took the occasion to see the group yesterday. I not only briefed them upon the structure of the Bureau and its accomplishments, but also dealt with some of the recent criticism which has been made of me personally and of the Bureau. I had no expectation that it would stir up as much publicity as it has. I realized, of course, that there would be articles in the various papers in the country, but I have been flooded today with telegrams from all sections of the country and out of the many hundreds that have been received, there have only been two or three which have criticized me for what I had to say about Martin Luther King. I share your view in thinking that his exposure is long overdue and maybe he is now beginning to get his just deserts. I certainly hope so.

It is grand to know that I have the support and goodwill of my close associates in the Bureau.

Sincerely,

Mr. William C. Sullivan
Federal Bureau of Investigation
Washington, D. C.

top lieutenant, condemning civil rights leader Martin Luther King Jr. It was Nov. 19, 1964, and Hoover the previous day had assailed King at a news conference as "the most notorious liar in the country." Now he was writing a colleague privately to say he hoped King was getting his "just deserts."

"I certainly hope so," Hoover wrote.

Four years later, King would be assassinated. And the letter — previously unknown to the public, a local author says — sheds yet more light on the historic malice the FBI director had toward King.

Washington scholar James L. Swanson said he found the letter inside an envelope clipped to a page in Hoover's 1938 book, "Persons in Hiding," which Swanson said he purchased in a bookstore several years ago.

This letter was written to the Deputy Director of the FBI and never mailed. It was found inside a book owned by J. Edgar Hoover, after his death.

The ending of the letter reflects Hoover's animosity toward Martin Luther King.

The harsh reality was: anyone liberal, a socialist, a union-supporter, black, or racially outspoken, was slapped with a 'communist' label so they could be dismissed, marginalized, investigated, prosecuted, or penalized.

Hoover's standard operating procedure was consistent.

THE BOMB HEARD AROUND THE WORLD

Chapter 14
THE INVESTIGATION CONTINUES

With J. Edgar Hoover as Director of the FBI commanding the most powerful investigative body in the country and being so heavily influenced by racial animus, prejudice, and bias, the likelihood of a balanced or fair investigation of the Harry and Harriette Moore assassinations was dubious.

Hoover's track record, where race was concerned, was problematic to say the least.

By summer of 1952 (6 months after the bombing) the NAACP publicly condemned the "failure of the county, state, and federal officials who, after more than six months, had proceeded no further than an investigation of the crime."

The NAACP passed a resolution which stated that the FBI was "almost invariably unable to cope with violent criminal action by bigoted, prejudiced Americans against Negro Americans."

By October, ten months after the bombing, Attorney General Howard McGrath announced that a federal grand jury in Miami began hearing testimony on the Florida bombings (Florida Terror), which would include the assassinations of Harry and Harriette Moore.

The first phase of the hearings focused solely on the Florida bombings in Miami, where forty-seven witnesses were subpoenaed including a dozen local Klansmen.

Ironically, December 9th, 1952, was the same day Thurgood Marshall faced the U.S. Supreme Court to begin oral arguments in the case of Brown vs. The Board of Education. The Federal Grand Jury in Miami finally handed down indictments in the Carver Village bombings against three Miami Klansmen. But per the FBI's jurisdictional limitations they were not charged for the bombings; instead they were charged with perjury only.

The Grand Jury reconvened on February 5 to hear testimony on the Moore case. Over thirty active or former Klansmen from Orlando, Winter Garden and Apopka were subpoenaed to testify.

"On March 25, after hearing from one hundred witnesses and thirty-two hundred pages of testimony, the Grand Jury issued a blistering twelve-page presentment on the Ku Klux Klan, describing it as a "cancerous growth ... founded on the worst instincts of mankind" and listing nineteen separate incidents—"a catalogue of terror that seems incredible" — committed by Klansmen in Miami and Orlando between 1943 and 1951. Their crimes ranged from murder and floggings to bombings and arson, fifteen of which occurred in the Orlando area, where the Klan appeared to be Running rampant."

KKK AND BOMBINGS

After looking at all other possibilities, the Ku Klux Klan became the focus of the FBI's investigation. The Klan was extremely active in Florida in the 1950's in Central Florida and the surrounding areas, including Mims (where the Moores were killed) and particularly in Lake County, Apopka, and Orlando.

FBI learned that it was standard for the Klan to recruit members from outside their communities or from nearby states to carry out their various terrorist activities.

They also learned that many high-ranking members of the community, including law enforcement officers, elected officials, and prominent business owners, were active members of the Klan or shared its beliefs or were sympathetic to same.

As mentioned earlier, the months leading up to the Moore bombing, there had been a series of terrorist Florida Terror bombings committed by the Klan throughout the state, and especially in the Miami area.

Racist assassins were nameless, faceless men of the hooded Klan, and any other white supremacist organizations in operation. Their crimes were public and, the inspiration for their crimes is understood. But Florida's governors, courts and, police officers were complicit, apathetic, or misguided.

After over a dozen bombings no one knew where the next bomb would explode.

The Tifereth Israel Synagogue had been bombed twice. At the crime scene, a Nazi swastika had been painted on a poster left behind to deliver the bombers' message.

It read in German...

"Achtung! Nieder Mit die Verdammte Juden und die Schmutzige Neger.

Signed: "Heil Hitler, K.K.K."

Translation...

"Attention! Down with the damned Jews and the dirty Negroes."

Signed: "Heil Hitler, K.K.K."

Resounding echoes of a not too distant past instilled terror in the hearts and minds and memories of many black and Jewish Americans. Strangely, not one newspaper, (at that time), suggested the Ku Klux Klan was a party of interest in the crimes.

At Harry T. Moore's funeral members of the Civil Rights Congress handed out pamphlets while Reverend Bruno held up a handful of letters and telegrams from around the world. Said the Reverend: "We have letters here from all over the United States, and from all over the world, from the other side of the ocean. The world knows why Mr. Moore died. The world honors Mr. Moore and, the world honors his message."

Sixteen white and black men and women from the North (from the Civil Rights Congress) flew South and stood among mourners. They arrived in the heart of the Klan country to speak for civilized Americans.

Meanwhile, outside the church, the representatives from the Civil Rights Congress distributed copies of their devastating indictment entitled: "We Charge Genocide."

It was delivered to the United Nations Assembly in France. The court of world opinion, it was hoped, would sit in judgment. And Jews, Catholics, and African Americans had no idea where domestic terrorists with bombs would strike next.

A black businessman in Miami interviewed by journalist, Joseph North, said this:

"Can you imagine what India feels when we say we are the bulwark of freedom? The Iranians? The Egyptians? Our country has become a laughing stock throughout the world with its pretensions to democracy. Mr. Patterson has introduced that charge of genocide at the United Nations. Mrs. Roosevelt denies genocide. Can her denial be believed when this is happening in Florida?"

Floridian government and citizens were deeply concerned as serial bombings continued in their communities. On December 9th, 1952 the American Jewish Congress accepted an invitation from the NAACP of Miami to co-sponsor a protest meeting at the Mt. Zion Baptist Church located in the black community.

Over 1200 whites and blacks came together to declare their horror and protest after the two black defendants in the Groveland case were shot by Sheriff Willis McCall and his lynch mob. And this group protested the violence against members of the Lake County community victimized by roving gangs of white residents and KKK members. As Harry Moore had done already, the twelve hundred demanded that Sheriff McCall be brought to justice.

This meeting was a landmark event for its time. These people came to this meeting, knowing that racist rogue bombers were still on the loose. They were there to take a stand.

Synagogues and Catholic churches were being bombed and in December of 1951, in Florida, Jewish war veterans volunteered to stand watch outside the meeting and patrol synagogues and churches in their own communities.

Three weeks later Harry and Harriette Moore were assassinated.

Florida newspapers declared that this new bombing, the one killing Harry and Harriette Moore, was not connected to the Miami bombings. Of course, this was pure conjecture and had no basis in fact. White-owned newspapers appeared to be attempting to maintain order in Miami.

The NAACP condemned Florida's law enforcement and government officials upon learning of the assassination of the Moores. Governor Fuller Warren shot back in the press, calling Walter White, NAACP Executive a "Harlem rabble-rouser for pay."

The realization was painfully clear. If you allow terrorists to kill blacks, Jews, Catholics, and dissenting Protestants, who is next. Freedom is indivisible. Withdraw it from one and; you withdraw from all. Jews had seen this methodology in action very recently.

To the Jews, Catholics, and blacks being attacked by serial bombings, it seemed that law enforcement consistently demonstrated their inability or their unwillingness to halt perpetrators and seek justice. A Jewish rabbi in Miami challenged Miami city authorities when he asked, "what good is government if it fails to protect the people who chose it?"

Over 'decent' America a pall of shame had settled.

For the assassinations of Harry and Harriette Moore more sermons were preached, more prayers offered, more resolutions adopted, more letters of protest arrived. But Florida and America were slow to respond.

Harry Moore's voter advocacy had become too effective and his success in registering and organizing black voters threatened existing political power structures where the Klan or white supremacist mentalities were entrenched.

The overwhelming consensus of most who were interviewed by FBI, Florida Department of Law Enforcement (FDLE), and Brevard County Sheriff's Office (BCSO) was that the Ku Klux Klan, and those affiliated, planted the bomb at Harry T. Moore's home.

FOUR MOTIVES

What reasons were there to harm Harry T. Moore? Law enforcement starts with motive. The FBI asked in 1951 and the FDLE revisited motives in 2004.

1. A year before Harry Moore's death, he had successfully launched a political campaign to defeat a twenty-year political boss of Brevard County named A. Fortenberry in his bid for reelection as Chairman of the County Commission.

TRANSCRIPTION OF A LETTER SENT TO
GOVERNOR WARREN ABOUT THE GROVELAND CASE

Governor Fuller Warren
State Capitol
Tallahassee, Florida

Dear Governor:

Sane-minded Florida citizens of all classes, creeds and colors must be shocked over recent developments in the famous Groveland Case. Despite the report of the coroner's jury that Sheriff McCall acted "in line of duty" when he shot Shepherd and Irvin, those fateful shots fired near Weirsdale on the night of Nov. 6th are still echoing around the world.

Thinking people naturally ask these questions: (1) In view of the mob action directed against those prisoners in 1949, was it safe to transport them into Lake County again with a guard of only two officers? (2) Did Sheriff McCall use sound judgment in attempting to drive his car and guard two prisoners at the same time? (3) Why did the officers follow a "blind" clay road after leaving Weirsdale? (4) If the prisoners did try to escape (which is extremely doubtful), was it necessary to shoot them four times in order to stop them, especially when they were handcuffed together? (5) Since the three Groveland boys had complained of severe beatings and inhuman treatment by Lake County officers in 1949, why were they permitted to leave Raiford again in custody of these same officers? (6) Is it true that the word of a Negro means nothing when weighed against that of a white person (as indicated by the three prisoners' complaints in 1949 and by Irvin's sworn statement last month)? (7) In the face of such strong evidence of gross neglect or willful intent to murder the prisoners, why have those officers not been suspended?

Yes, these questions are too important to be ignored. We need not try to "whitewash" this case or bury our heads in the sand, like an ostrich. Florida is on trial before the rest of the world. Only prompt and courageous action by you in removing these officers can save the good name of our fair state. We also repeat our request for ample and constant State guard for Irvin in future hearings on this case.

Florida Negro citizens are still mindful of the fact that our votes proved to be your margin of victory in the 2nd primary of 1948. We seek no special favors; but certainly we have a right to expect justice and equal protection of the laws even for the humblest Negro. Shall we be disappointed again?

Respectfully yours,
(signed Harry T. Moore)
Harry T. Moore, Executive Secretary
Progressive Voters' League of Florida

Harry had registered a remarkable group of black voters in that district. An unheard of amount of African Americans had been registered totaling nearly fifty-one percent.

Harry worked tirelessly for a man named Dave Nisbet, in what ought to have been a losing battle. Precisely because of Harry's efforts, the voting results delivered a stunning upset in favor of underdog, Nisbet.

Whites and traditional southern conservatives were astonished and very bitter. After Fortenberry's upsetting defeat, everyone in the political power structure became sharply aware of Harry Moore as a viable political threat.

2. Weeks before Harry's death, he launched an aggressive campaign aimed at Sheriff Willis McCall, law enforcement, the courts, and the government.

He was vocal and aggressive about outrageous injustices perpetrated on the four African Americans framed for the Groveland alleged rape of a white woman. He called for Sheriff McCall, the controversial sheriff of Lake County, to be indicted for his violent racist behavior throughout the legal process.

In point of fact, there was very little about the process that actually was legal, with beatings of the defendants to get confessions, the terrorizing of the black community for crimes which never happened, the hunting down and slaughtering of one of the four defendants, and the shootings of two other handcuffed black prisoners being transported by McCall for retrial.

And then there was the all-white jury instructed by a white judge who had
no interest in justice for the African American defendants. This was 'legal' by
their standards - but in actuality it was another form of lynching.

3. NAACP tensions mounted with Harry's aggressive political and community activities in Florida. He devoted a great deal of time to voter registration,
his Progressive Voters' League, and seminars to educate blacks about the
process.

Black voters registration

And he continued his activities against race crimes, but according to the NAACP, he was not fulfilling the needs of the NAACP. They pleaded financial issues were making it difficult to keep Harry on salary, and allegedly, they wanted him to bring in more revenue for the NAACP in Florida.

Four weeks before his death, Harry was removed from his position as Executive Secretary, with the NAACP owing him sizable back wages. Harry was invested professionally and personally and was hurt by their abandonment, but he had put too much into his relationships to walk away. So he volunteered to work without pay as State Coordinator for the NAACP.

This situation was tenuous at best; they were not supporting his efforts, and he had no other means of support except for Harriette's commuting to a teaching job out of town. After his death, the NAACP offered to provide a decent amount of funding to Harriette Moore to assist with burial costs and family expenses.

They offered a much smaller amount at her deathbed.

Union Organizer in Florida

4. And there were other motives which also made Harry a target. Moore was (allegedly) influencing black citrus grove workers to organize a union. If they did, wages and demands would have to be addressed and amended. White company owners would not tolerate this.

Harry had started a small orange grove around his home (which consisted of ten acres of land.) Some grove owners thought Harry could also lure black grove workers to come to work for him with better wages.

Harry T. Moore was not only outspoken; he was a threat on nearly every possible level to the white business community, law enforcement, the courts, and to the government.

Chapter 15
UPPITY OR EQUAL

"Uppity" was a word unique to the South. If an African American was successful, outspoken, or too confident, he was 'uppity'.

White southerners were offended and often took action against blacks who were this way.

Black people who were "too big for their britches" were often kidnapped and taken to secret locations to be given the "treatment". They would be beaten or whipped, or tortured in horrific ways. Some were beaten so brutally that they would not survive. Some were murdered outright.

The KKK was so bold in enforcing its beliefs that many of these acts of terrorism were carried out in broad daylight on public city streets, in full view. The idea was to instill fear in those who viewed the horrors.

By comparison, in pre-war Germany, Hitler's 'brown shirt militia' roamed the streets of Berlin, doing precisely the same thing to Jews. It was an effective way to create an environment of terror causing the public to recoil in fear for themselves and their families.

As evidence leaked to confirm that Governor Fuller Warren had been a former Klansman, many law enforcement officers attended Klan meetings in full uniform. Their membership boasted political leaders, businesspeople, attorneys, doctors, government officials, and prominent members of the Florida community.

Harry Moore faced formidable odds.

When the trial came to an examination of the assassinations of Harry and Harriette Moore, there was no traction, whatsoever. The grand jury laid the blame for their deaths on the Orlando-area Klan, which was "known to have evidenced a malevolent interest in Moore." But evidence was not sufficient to indict. And no charges were ever filed.

During the trial newspaper clippings about Moore had allegedly been read at Klan meetings and, a most startling revelation, the floor plan of Harry T. Moore's house had reportedly been exhibited at a Klan meeting in Apopka. Whoever bombed the Moore home knew precisely where to place the bomb to do maximum damage. Having a floor plan would be mandatory and the KKK had one. There were no indictments.

In June, the grand jury handed down seven indictments against Orlando-area Klansmen, but only for perjury pertaining to the Florida Terror bombings.

No mention was made of the Moore bombing.

At the defendants' arraignment on June 19, defense attorney Edgar Waybright, Jr., of Jacksonville, (a Klan officer himself), filed a motion to quash all the current indictments because the federal grand jury had no local jurisdiction in the State of Florida. These were state crimes, not federal, so a federal grand jury had 'no authority.' Two months later, in December 1953, Judge George Whitehurst threw out all the indictments against the Klan's five defendants who had been charged with perjury.

Both cases under investigation were directly connected to active members of the Ku Klux Klan, or those who were associated, sympathetic, or related. By the end of the investigation dozens of Florida citizens were indicted (but only for civil rights violations and perjury) and not for the bombings.

No one was ever indicted for the assassinations of Harry and Harriette Moore. It seemed that the FBI's only strategy was to charge individuals with the lesser crimes in hopes of 'turning' people who may want to make deals and provide additional useful information along the way about the Moore or Florida Terror bombings.

The maximum penalty for a civil rights violation was one year plus a possible small fine. After four years of FBI investigation, no one was prosecuted.

While the FBI committed enormous resources to the investigation, the fact that Mr. Hoover was 'running the investigation' throws suspicion on its outcome. His predisposition against African Americans, his bias, lack of sensitivity and disrespect for other races, his arrogance, and his anti-liberal views could have impacted the investigation in a multitude of ways. There were many negative opinions of the FBI investigation once the final results of both cases were tallied.

Most called the investigation into the Moore killings a fraud. Author and undercover investigative journalist, Stetson Kennedy labeled it a conspiracy. Still others felt justice could never have been delivered based on the parties investigating the crimes.

The same was said of the lack of transparency and justice pertaining to the Florida Terror bombings.

After that, the American public (not so much in the South), the news media, NAACP, and an army of American civil rights organizations denounced the investigation's lack of results with a vengeance. But as news cycles go, it all faded into history. What could anyone do? Besides, in 1954, the Supreme Court Decision of the Brown vs. The Board of Education overshadowed everything. "Separate but Equal" was no longer.

The country was in an uproar - and the bombings of Harry and Harriette Moore, Jewish Synagogues, Catholic Churches, Jewish and Catholic schools, business, and civil rights offices faded into history.

And five years had passed since the charge of 'genocide' at the United Nations.

Eleanor Roosevelt was right about one thing. The history of racial murders in America symbolized by the killings of Harry and Harriette Moore and their deaths made a poignant statement around the world. Harry and Harriette Moore symbolized the 'new civil rights' movement, for all intents and purposes, and they were 'the first out of the gate.' Once segregation was outlawed, many African Americans offered their voices. But Harry T. Moore had been on a perilous journey, alone, and unprotected.

Justice in America, it seemed, was not possible, at least not for blacks or minorities. The Moore assassinations further deepened mistrust of the justice system, its representatives, its legal system, its law enforcement, its judicial system, and the nation's constitution.

The Moore case was officially dead; so was the Florida Terror bombing case. America, the land of liberty, had a dark cloud hanging overhead. And it has never really gone away.

SEPARATE BUT EQUAL

"Separate but equal" is a phrase most of us have heard before, however, it is imperative that we understand and acknowledge the impact of the Supreme Court decision that created this ideology and this policy.

In 1896, the Supreme Court of the United States ruled in the Plessy vs. Ferguson Decision that <u>racially segregated public facilities were legal,</u> so long as the facilities for blacks and whites were equal.

The Supreme Court institutionalized discrimination in America in 1896.

With this decision the Supreme Court confirmed that blacks and whites were not required to mix, and that white citizens could not be forced to mingle, or interact, or learn with, or share with, or eat with, or travel with, or live side-by-side with African Americans. The Supreme Court launched 'segregation' as an American policy and ideology by which Americans could live openly and legally.

It was a defining moment for the country, and an astonishingly, racist decision. It set America on a grim path which severely impacted the nation, and does so to this day. Once again similarities to the infamous racist laws set forth by "apartheid" enacted in South Africa are alarming.

Apartheid was established in South Africa as policy of segregation and discrimination on the basis of race. Apartheid comes from the Afrikaans definition which means **'apartness'**. In 1948, the National Party in South Africa implemented this ideology which called for separate development of blacks and whites in South Africa.

South Africa's apartheid ideology 'smacked' of America's Supreme Court Decision, Plessy vs. Ferguson from 1896. The language of the Apartheid legislation, upon its reading, appeared to have come from the American playbook. South Africa's version called for equal development and freedom of cultural expression for blacks, but instead it forced them to live in dire conditions, oppressed, starved, and abused in every possible way.

The American version essentially offered the same. The alleged 'equality' of the facilities the Supreme Court referred to was fictitious, (as in South Africa). It reinforced the notion that America's blacks should also live in a dire economic system, oppressed, starved, and abused in every possible way.

There never was equality; not in any venue, locale, facility, not in schools, transportation, business, restaurants, bus stops, drinking fountains, beaches, parks, playgrounds, the military, or anywhere in American society.

The actual point of Plessy vs. Ferguson was to keep blacks and whites separated; to keep blacks 'in their place'. The Supreme Court provided a national home for "Jim Crow" laws.

BROWN VS. THE BOARD OF EDUCATION

In the 1950s, the National Association for the Advancement of Colored People had worked hard to challenge segregation laws in public schools and had filed lawsuits on behalf of plaintiffs in states South Carolina, Virginia and Delaware.

Protesters march against school segregation.

In the case that would become most famous, a plaintiff named Oliver Brown filed a class-action suit against the Board of Education of Topeka, Kansas, in 1951, after his daughter, Linda Brown, was denied entrance to Topeka's all-white elementary schools.

In his lawsuit, Brown claimed that schools for black children were not equal to the white schools and that segregation violated the so-called "equal protection clause" of the 14th Amendment, which holds that no state can "deny to any person within its jurisdiction the equal protection of the laws."

The case went before the U.S. District Court in Kansas, which agreed that public school segregation had a "detrimental effect upon the colored children" and contributed to "a sense of inferiority," but still upheld the "separate but equal" doctrine.

In 1954, all of America had shifted its gaze to the Brown vs. The Board of Education Supreme Court Decision, handed down May 17th, 1954.

It halted white supremacists' insidious actions, beginning with education. But many southern states angrily vowed they would not comply with this new 'federal law.' Some Southern states even threatened to secede if integration was forced on them. The South was determined to maintain their segregationist policies.

And people like Sheriff Willis McCall were front and center in the bid to ignore the new law.

Brown vs. Board of Education of Topeka was a landmark Supreme Court case in which the justices ruled, unanimously, that racial segregation of children in public schools was unconstitutional. An addendum to the law came later, banning businesses from segregation, as well.

This Supreme Court decision was the cornerstone of the civil rights movement and helped establish the precedent that "separate-but-equal" education and other services were not equal at all.

Plessy vs. Ferguson was finally nullified by the Supreme Court Decision of Brown vs. The Board of Education, in 1954. However, the decision was not fully recognized, enforced, or enacted (at least in the South) until 1965.

To the great disappointment of segregationists, the Brown Decision eliminated segregation in America. 'Separate but equal' was no more. It changed the country, and it needed changing.

A seamstress from a department store, named Rosa Parks, refused to give up her seat on the bus to a white passenger. She was immediately arrested for civil disobedience, violating Alabama segregation laws. Her courageous act launched the year-long Montgomery bus boycott that would become the civil rights movement's first great triumph and make a national celebrity out of its leader, an unknown young preacher named Martin Luther King Jr.

Rosa Parks' act of so-called disobedience inspired the African American community to support her actions and boycott Montgomery buses for an entire year. Her defiance of Alabama's segregation laws occurred after the Supreme Court had ruled. The South certainly did not want the Federal government to tell them how to live their lives.

They wanted their blacks to continue living in a segregated society as they had always done, legally, since 1896, and day-to-day for centuries before that.

Civil rights had become a viable tool to challenge the white-dominated system. And Rosa Parks became an icon for freedom and desegregation around the world. She really did upset the fictitious "tranquility of the South."

And while this appears to be, in retrospect, a remarkable success story, it came with a price. After Rosa Parks' challenged Alabama and the white-run system there, she lost her job and received death threats for many years after.

After the decision, most Southern states were so displeased that State Congressmen passed opposing legislation to the Supreme Court decision which dismissed Brown vs. The Board of Education, called the "Southern Manifesto', allowing segregation to continue.

But eventually, under President Lyndon Johnson, the Civil Rights Act of 1964 and the Voting Rights Act of 1965 finally dismantled institutional segregation.

Chief Justice Earl Warren's Court made the decision which is viewed as the start of the Civil Rights Movement and this is, in part, why Harry T. Moore

Chief Justice Earl Warren's Court

has not been fully recognized or accredited for his remarkable civil rights and human rights efforts. He was many years ahead of his time.

After the Supreme Court's desegregation decision, a White Citizens Council organized in Mississippi, which invited Florida's infamous Sheriff Willis McCall to be the Director of the National Association for the Advancement of White People.

McCall was in his 'racist wheelhouse.' At a convention in the State of Delaware, he announced to five thousand supporters that they should all oppose integration. His actual words were: "Go to it."

Upon his return to Florida, McCall's interview at the Tampa Tribune illustrated his intentions accurately:

Willis McCall: *"I, for one, am going to do all I can to forestall such a movement (referring to integration). I am one who, instead of sitting around grumbling about agitators, goes into action. We need more action and not so much wishie-washie grumbling."*

During the next year, after the Brown Decision, the national civil rights movement would be born. Outrage over the August 1955 murder in Mississippi

of fourteen-year-old Emmett Till, (for whistling at a white girl), gave the embryonic movement a jump-start and, four months later, Rosa Parks actions.

As desegregation took hold, the battle moved to Birmingham, Nashville, Tallahassee, Little Rock, Greensboro, and many other cities in the south.

And the unsolved assassinations of Harry and Harriette Moore seemed to be forgotten. Assassins were out there living their lives and nothing was being done. Evangeline and Annie Moore had to endure sadness and heartache with little hope of justice in sight.

"Those who deny freedom to others, deserve it not for themselves"
~ Abraham Lincoln

"Slaves working in 17th Century Virginia" Unknown artist, 1670

"Better to die fighting for freedom then be a prisoner all the days of your life."
∽ Bob Marley

AFRICAN AMERICANS IN AMERICA

Unbeknownst to most Americans, blacks had been in America for centuries before it existed as a country. They arrived in what was then called La Florida, under Spanish rule, long before the Puritans came. Sadly, blacks were treated savagely, before America was formed -- and worse after.

"To put this in perspective, people of African heritage were among the first foreigners to the shores of La Florida and North America, and they achieved this over one-hundred years prior to the settlement of the Pilgrims and Puritans in New England...under Spanish rule, and later under British rule, faced political and social restrictions from the earliest contact that sought to reduce them to servitude. From the advent of the Spanish notions of inferiority and race-based oppression, blacks originated and sustained a freedom struggle that would last in Florida under different regimes, political entities, and social conditions for almost five centuries." ∽ Florida's Freedom Struggle

Between 1882 and 1964, approximately four thousand people died from lynching.

The 1890s witnessed the worst period of lynching in U.S. history. Lynchings, often seen by large crowds of white onlookers, were the most extreme form of Southern white control over the African-American population, regularly imposed on African Americans who had been falsely charged with crimes but in fact, were achieving a level of political or economic autonomy that whites found unacceptable.

The history of failed attempts to pass federal anti-lynching legislation goes back to 1894 when a House bill to set up a committee to investigate lynchings failed. In 1922, the House passed a bill to make lynching a Federal crime, but despite President Warren G. Harding's support, Southern senators filibustered and defeated it.

In 1933, President Franklin D. Roosevelt failed to support an anti-lynching bill proposed by the NAACP, fearing that key Southern lawmakers would retaliate and interfere with his New Deal agenda. Politics superseded human values at every turn.

In February 1948, President Harry S. Truman asked Congress for federal anti-lynching legislation. In the following testimony to a House sub-committee, four Southern Congressmen discussed their reasons for opposing what they deemed Federal interference in state judicial responsibilities and defend segregation and the "peaceful relations now existing between white man and Negro" in the South.

None of the bills under consideration by the subcommittee passed.

> *"For years the Western academic and scientific establishment has claimed that Black people are small-brained, genetically inferior subhumans with no history. This has been devastating to the self-esteem of people of African descent in general and Black children in particular."*

> ∼ David Imhotep, Ph.D. *(The First Americans Were Africans)*

Chapter 16

FOUR INVESTIGATIONS
1951 • 1978 • 1991 • 2004

(DOJ SOURCE)
VICTIMS HARRY AND HARRIETTE MOORE

Harry T. Moore:
Born in Houston, Florida. DOB 11/18/1905, died 12/25/1951.
Parents: S. Johnny and Rosalea Alberta Tyson Moore. Only child.
Graduated from Florida Memorial High School, Live Oak, 1925.
Graduated from Bethune Cookman College with a
Normal Degree in 1936 and a BA degree in 1951.

∽

Harriette V. Moore
Born in West Palm Beach, Florida. DOB 06/19/1902, died 01/03/1952.
Sisters: Valerie Simms, Mae Mebane; brothers: George Simms,
Arnold Simms, Rupert Simms, David Simms

∽

1. The first investigation into the assassinations of Harry T. and Harriette
   V. Moore was coordinated by the FBI and commenced in the early morning hours after the explosion in 1951.

2. The second investigation in 1978 was a joint investigation run by the
   Brevard County Sheriff's Office working with the Brevard County State
   Attorney's Office.

3. The third investigation in 1991 was initiated by the Florida Department
   of Law Enforcement ("FDLE"), under then-Governor Lawton Chiles.

4. The fourth investigation in 2004 was launched by the Florida Attorney
   General Charlie Crist through the Office of Civil Rights working with
   FDLE.

1951
FBI INVESTIGATION

*At approximately 3:05 AM the FBI arrived to commence the initial
investigation into the assassinations of Harry T. and Harriette V. Moore.*

The FBI investigation began 4.5 hours after the explosion and continued through 1955. Nearly eighty FBI agents conducted over
1,500 interviews in five states: Florida, Georgia, North Carolina, South
Carolina, and California. FBI collected evidence through telephones and
surveillance, as well as forensic analysis of physical evidence (although
forensics in that era were primitive by today's standards).

The first information the FBI had to assess and manage was the wave of
gossip and speculation circulating throughout the state. Many persons
of interest were investigated, including Moore family members, NAACP
executives, neighbors, police officers, political candidates, school board
executives, store owners, teachers, students, business associates, citrus farm
owners, and Ku Klux Klan members.

The FBI did not, at first, consider seriously that elected officials could be
suspects in these killings, but it was a fact that Governor Fuller Warren
had been an active member of the Klan. And J.J. Eliot, Warren's right
hand, and special investigator had been accused of being an active Klan
member.

Many other officials of the Florida court system and law enforcement were
also active Klan members. (Some officials allegedly attended Klan rallies
in their uniforms.)

And a city official running for office just before Moore's death. A.
Fortenberry, lost the election solely because Harry T. Moore's 'block voting'
strategy was effective. There were suspects aplenty and many with motives,
too.

Meanwhile, Harriette Moore (while on her deathbed in the hospital)
instructed FBI agents to examine all Lake County officials seriously. These
officials were unanimously hostile toward Harry Moore, and most of

them were in the Klan, too. Those who were not active members had friends or family in the Klan or had sympathies and connections to the organization.

The Groveland case (in Lake County) was a nightmare, and still in progress at the time of the Moore bombing. It was the kind of story you read about in a Harper Lee novel or view in a motion picture, and never want to believe it could have happened.

The Groveland Four case was a travesty of justice. The Supreme Court agreed and overturned the convictions of the defendants. The re-trial was set for 1952. Four blacks had been indicted: one was underage and pled guilty to a lesser sentence, the other was hunted down by a posse and shot to death). The remaining two were transported for the retrial and shot by Sheriff McCall, en route.

Moore was so outraged that he wrote to Governor Warren and law enforcement officials calling for McCall to be charged with murder.

McCall had reportedly been investigated dozens of times for civil rights violations, racial violence, and murders. But to white Floridians, McCall's behavior and actions seemed to matter less than the outrageous actions of a black man calling for the indictment of a respected white sheriff.

Numerous witnesses, including Harry's family and co-workers, believed his activities in the Groveland case were directly responsible for his death and that Sheriff McCall was directly involved. The FBI could not find a link to connect McCall to the murders.

The FBI took over the initial investigation from state law enforcement. The bombing of the Moore's home was handled as a 'civil rights crime' and not as a murder (for which FBI had no jurisdiction in Florida.)

Once the FBI's focus turned to the Klan, the FBI identified two suspects: Klansmen Earl J. Brooklyn and Tillman H. Belvin. Both had reputations for extreme violence and were allegedly expelled from the Georgia Klan for same. They rejoined the KKK in Florida.

Brooklyn and Belvin had a pattern of participating in attacks on minorities, mostly blacks. Both were members of the Apopka and Winter Garden Klaverns of the KKK and, both had been members of the Association of Georgia Klans. FBI Special Agents interviewed Brooklyn and Belvin.

Before the bombing, Brooklyn allegedly had a current floor plan of Harry Moore's house and shared it with other Klan members at meetings. A paid FBI informant testified that "I will say this, he (Brooklyn) did tell me (the informant) at that time that the bombing was done in Mims by members of the Orlando unit." The FBI asked: "By members of the Orlando Klavern?" The informant answered "Yes." The informant stated that he was quite sure that he reported his conversation with Brooklyn to the FBI.

And a witness identified Brooklyn and Belvin after they visited a local store to ask for directions to the Moore home. Finally, when interviewed by the FBI, Earl Brooklyn, could not account for his actions on Christmas night, 1951. His family offered conflicting accounts as to his movements the night of the bombing.

The FBI reported later that a Klan member contacted the second person of interest, Tillman Belvin, in January to inquire about obtaining dynamite. Belvin's reply was: "No, I used it all on the last job."

While all of this is hearsay, or at least not conclusive, it does create an evocative thumbnail view of possible events leading to the deaths of the Moores.

Belvin was also known to wear a size six shoe, and his size footprint was found at the scene of the explosion. In today's forensic science, law enforcement likely could have identified the shoe's sole imprint precisely, based on soil samples and sole patterns, but in the 1950's they did not have the science.

Four days before the bombing, Belvin allegedly paid off the balance of his mortgage, approximately $2500 (which was a healthy sum in 1951).

But now there was another name: Joseph Neville Cox. He was also a Klansman whose name was shared with them through an FBI informant. Perhaps Cox could provide information about Belvin and Brooklyn.

The FBI interviewed him. He freely admitted that he was a former Klansman connected with the Association of Georgia Klans in Orlando. Cox stated that he dropped active participation in the Klan because he was involved in politics. At the time of this interview, Cox was running for the office of Supervisor of Elections for Orange County.

Cox disavowed knowledge of Klan members being involved in terrorist activities although he admitted that it was possible that the Klan might have been involved in beatings (beatings were called "rides"). He claimed he had no knowledge of the Moore bombing.

But Cox admitted that Tillman Belvin was "quite a radical person a few years ago, but at the present time, Belvin is a very sick man and has not been associated with the Klan in any way since the beginning of World War II." He also knew Brooklyn but refused to elaborate on their activities because of his Klan oath.

On March 29, 1952, FBI Special Agents re-interviewed Joseph Neville Cox in Orlando. Cox, employed by the Medlock Tractor Company, advised that he left the Association of Georgia Klans two years prior and joined the Southern Knights of the Ku Klux Klan.

Cox stated that he did not have any Klan records and that when the Association of Georgia Klans changed to the Southern Knights of the Ku Klux Klan, records were destroyed. Cox once again denied knowing Moore and would not provide information concerning Klansmen.

However, he continually asked FBI Special Agents if the evidence the FBI now had would hold up in court. The FBI Special Agents told him the evidence would hold up in court.

The next day, on March 30, 1952, Joseph Neville Cox committed suicide at his residence in Winter Garden at 11:30 A. M. Winter Garden Police Chief Carl Buchanan advised that Cox did not leave a suicide note and that Cox's family was unable to offer any explanation for his suicide. It was particularly odd because Cox had no medical or financial problems and he was preparing to run for public office as Supervisor of Elections for Orange County.

Police Chief Carl Buchanan investigated Cox's suicide. If he had left a suicide note confessing to the Moore bombing as a reason for suicide, it would likely have been destroyed by Buchanan. Buchanan was also Klansman.

FBI STRATEGY

By spring of 1952, the FBI knew its investigation was not going to produce results. They were getting nowhere.

The Bureau revised its strategy to attempt to indict Klansmen (not for civil rights) but for 'perjury' based on many Klansmen making false statements on federal employment applications concerning individual membership in the Klan. As well they hoped to indict Klansmen who lied to FBI Special Agents about being members of a terrorist organization.

The Bureau had determined that several members of the Ku Klux Klan may have violated Title 18, Section 20 of the United States Code, in that they answered "no" on their federal employment application (Form number 57) which asked if "the applicant had ever been convicted of a crime or that the applicant belonged to any organization which advocated the overthrow of the U. S. Government or "was seeking by force and violence to deny other persons their rights under the Constitution of the United States."

Unfortunately, it didn't work. In January of 1955, perjury charges were dismissed by the U. S. District Court in Orlando. By September of the same year U. S. Attorney, James L. Gilmartin, closed the Moore case effective August 19, 1955, since the statute of limitations had run out, and no evidence was available to show any violation of Harriette or Harry Moore's civil rights.

August 17, 1955, after the United States Federal Court in Miami, dismissed all charges of perjury against Klansmen, The U. S. Attorney's Office filed a petition of Certiorari with the United States Supreme Court. The U. S. Supreme Court declined certiorari (a writ or order by which a higher court reviews a decision of a lower court) on May 9, 1955.

The FBI presented evidence to a federal grand jury in the Moore investigation and, seven individual Klan members were indicted for perjury. The Federal court dismissed the indictments.

When the U. S. Attorney's Office closed its investigation on August 19, 1955, the physical evidence, according to FBI records, was turned over to the Brevard County Sheriff's Office.

That evidence disappeared and was never recovered.

How could evidence from a four-year federal investigation of such enormous importance disappear? The Brevard County Sheriff's Office indicated the evidence was lost or misplaced. According to the FBI and FDLE reports, the missing evidence vanished without a trace.

On studying this case and these events in this era, that crucial evidence in a Federal and State criminal case collected by the most esteemed law enforcement organizations in both the country and the state can disappear is unfathomable.

The FBI committed four years of intensive labor, consisting of over 1500 interviews employing 78 Special Agents and amassing physical evidence gathered from five states, with thousands of pages of investigative notes, and the physical evidence from the crime scene.

Luckily FBI Special Agents had corresponded regularly with Hoover and the home office support team. Some files still existed in Washington, but the physical evidence had gone missing with thousands of pages of investigatory work product.

This reality provides another layer of mistrust in the legal and law enforcement process operating in the 1950's. Injustice lurks around every corner.

Much of the evidence the FBI did collect in the Harry T. Moore case was circumstantial but, even so, that preponderance of evidence did not earn Brooklyn and Belvin indictment status. And it provided considerable crucial information, context, and invaluable data needed to assess and further investigate the assassinations, their supporters, possible conspirators, and local law enforcement which may or may not have collaborated.

Regarding the 'prime suspects,' strangely, both Brooklyn and Belvin died during the FBI investigation. Belvin died of natural causes in August 1952 while Brooklyn died of natural causes on Christmas Day, 1952, precisely one year to the day after the Moore bombing.

The FBI had not finished their inquiry at this time and, evidence they did have was not sufficient to charge or indict. They were in pursuit of the assassins, but legally they could only indict for civil rights violations or later, perjury.

The purpose of the FBI investigation and strategy comes into question here. The FBI could not bring the killers to justice directly for the crimes which they committed.

Accordingly, the apparent rationale was to charge suspects for civil rights violations and hope that violators would 'turn' on the actual killers. Civil rights violations in that era carried a fine (of approximately $100.00) and little prison time if any. It would hardly have been a productive inducement for anyone to have turned on anyone in a criminal case.

The initial investigation had the most promising window of time in which to find the perpetrators.

One wonders why there was not a dual investigation launched to allow state authorities to pursue the Moore assassins, while FBI pursued civil rights violations?

It is true that state authorities were not well-regarded where racial crime investigations were concerned; however, a dual investigation could have, at very least, provided a cross-check between two levels of law enforcement, where sharing of resources might have benefited both organizations. All parties are gone now and, there is no one to ask. But the situation still begs the question.

There are likely technical and jurisdictional answers to be had with a number of these queries, but common sense and logic appear to have been abandoned.

Instead, there was the either-or approach. The FBI investigation offered a 'don't trust state law enforcement' to pursue killers; but 'do trust federal enforcement' to pursue civil rights violators.

These were odd choices. Given the importance of the crimes, this approach did not create an opportunity for justice to be served. And it wasn't.

As we look back on this, decades later, this was not so much a pursuit of justice, as it was a pursuit of political expediency.

Another way to say this, from an outsider's point of view: it appears to be a systemic failure on a grand scale.

1978
BCSO INVESTIGATION

Brevard County Sherriff's Office (BCSO) and County
State Attorney's Office Investigation

It was Brevard County Sheriff Roland Zimmerman who reopened the Moore murders investigation. He was inspired after attending one of the many memorial services held for the late Harry Moore.

One detective was assigned from the Brevard County Sheriff's Office ("BCSO") to retrace the steps of the initial FBI investigation. Shortly after that, complaints poured in to complain that one detective hardly qualifies as the 'reopening' of a case of this magnitude. Four additional investigators were assigned.

During that investigation, a resident, Edward L. Spivey called the BCSO to complain about the renewed interest in this closed case. He was, allegedly perturbed that law enforcement was re-examining the assassinations.

Spivey attacked the Brevard County Sherriff's Office's (BCSO) efforts for wasting taxpayer dollars. The BCSO soon learned that Spivey was a former high-ranking member of the Ku Klux Klan in central Florida.

A BCSO detective working the case interviewed Spivey. Suspiciously, Spivey revealed precise details of the Moore bombing which were too precise. That investigator recorded the interviews.

Spivey finally revealed that his close friend, Joseph Cox, was responsible for detonating the bomb under the Moore home. He also alleged that the Klan had not sanctioned Cox to do the bombing. Spivey was dying of cancer. The BCSO detective considered the interviews with Spivey to be 'deathbed' confessions. Spivey was angry about the FBI interviews with Cox. He blamed the FBI for Cox committing suicide. And he hated blacks. He had no remorse about Moore and his wife.

Belvin, Brooklyn, and Cox were a trio linked together. Spivey indicated Cox had arthritis so he would have needed help to do the bombing. As well,

Belvin had the right size footprint, based on footprints at the crime scene. Spivey provided between six and ten confessions in his many interviews.

Joseph Cox, also a member of the Ku Klux Klan, had been investigated during the FBI's initial investigation. He was known to be an active member of the Klan and, as mentioned earlier, the FBI questioned him twice, as a person of interest in the assassinations.

Through the Cox interviews, FBI was looking for information about the two original suspects, Brooklyn and Belvin. Cox was first interviewed by the FBI on March 10, 1952, and denied knowledge of the bombing. The FBI report indicates he was helpful in providing background on the two suspects, Brooklyn and Belvin.

The second interview on March 29, 1952, had Cox, once again, denying any knowledge of the bombing.

The next day Joseph Cox committed suicide. He killed himself with a shotgun borrowed from his friend, Spivey. Committing suicide the day after an FBI interview is not a subtle response to an interview with law enforcement.

While it does not prove he was 'the bomber' of the Moore home, his suicide speaks volumes as to the likelihood that he was involved. We'll never know.

Winter Garden Police investigated the suicide. Cox allegedly did not leave a suicide note, but the Winter Garden Police were known for their KKK connections and sympathies. There may well have been a note.

Spivey informed the BCSO that Cox came to his house the day after Cox's second interview with the FBI and admitted to Spivey that he "had done something wrong."

Cox admitted using the money to pay off some debts (his mortgage). Spivey surmised that Cox was frightened that the FBI would learn of his paying off his mortgage debt. Cox borrowed Spivey's shotgun and returned home where he committed suicide.

It was twenty-seven years after the assassinations of Harry and Harriette Moore the BCSO discovered this information.

Prosecutors from the Brevard County State Attorney's Office attended several of the Spivey interviews. Spivey's accounts of the bombing and its execution were so detailed that the BCSO trusted Spivey's account of the crime, so much so, that they not only believed Cox planted the bomb, but that Spivey was in attendance; that he participated.

Sadly, the State Attorney, Douglas Cheshire, while preparing to indict Spivey, lost his bid for reelection.

Spivey was never prosecuted and the case closed. Spivey died of cancer.

1991 FDLE INVESTIGATION
The 1991 Florida Department of Law Enforcement Investigation

In 1991, the Governor of Florida, Lawton Chiles, ordered the Florida Department of Law Enforcement ("FDLE") to investigate only new information regarding the bombing. FDLE was not to re-visit material that had been investigated in the two prior investigations.

The re-opening of the case was, in part, motivated by a report from a Klan member's wife claiming her husband told her that he took part in the Harry Moore bombing.

The FDLE interviewed the former KKK member. He admitted to being a member of the Klan but denied any knowledge being involved in the bombing. He later passed a lie detector test. However, author and journalist, Stetson Kennedy, was not impressed with the manner in which the investigation had been managed.

Based on the dismissive behavior to which he was subjected, he had an unfavorable outlook on this new investigation.

Below is the NY Times article penned by Stetson Kennedy, upon learning Governor Lawton Chiles of Florida re-opened the case. The precise text of the article is revealing.

It was thus hardly surprising that instead of indicting anyone for more serious charges, the grand jury came up only with perjury indictments for 12 Ku Klux Klan members.

Even at a time when civil rights laws were virtually nonexistent, the court's dismissal required the studious suppression of all evidence implicating law officers in the conspiracy.

Frank Meech, a retired F.B.I. agent who had played a leading role in the original probe, said in an October television interview: "There was a general feeling in the law enforcement community at that time that Harry T. Moore had gotten too big for his britches and had to go." He added, that "for the tranquility of the South, and all, it was decided not to prosecute."

Another guest on the show was the retired Lake County sheriff, Willis McCall, who seven weeks before the killing had shot his gun into two black prisoners handcuffed together.

Asked about accusations that he had bankrolled the Moore assassinations, Mr. McCall said with a smirk, "I would have, but I didn't have that kind of money."

Stetson Kennedy stated: If Mr. Chiles makes good on his promise to follow the trail to its end, he will likely discover that the Moore murders were carefully planned, carefully carried out and, with the F.B.I.'s help, carefully covered up."

The FDLE then examined the validity of a 1978 confession from Raymond Henry, a previous suspect in the FBI investigation. In his confession, Henry claimed that he was hired to make the bomb and carry out the crime, and he identified four other individuals as involved.

Members of the FDLE interviewed Henry twice. During these interviews, he essentially recanted his 1978 confession, admitting it was a lie based on rumor, speculation and hearsay. Sources confirmed that much information provided by Henry in 1978 was not credible.

Finally, the FDLE researched rumors concerning the possible involvement of Sheriff McCall, as well as a group of Klansmen known as the "Sydney Walker Hopper Group," in the Moore murders. No evidence was obtained that would link either McCall or the "Sydney Walker Hopper Group" to the crimes. The FDLE's March 24, 1992, Investigative Summary indicated that the FDLE was unable to prove Ms. Harrington's claims and they were able to discredit Raymond Henry's "confession."

The Governor Lawton Chiles' investigation of 1991 closed without any result.

FLORIDA'S CHRISTMAS MURDERS
(NY TIMES - ARCHIVES 1991)

This transcription of the New York Times editorial from author Stetson Kennedy, in 1991, reflects his dismay with and criticism of the FBI investigation and the follow-up with the Brevard County investigation in 1978.

Page in Time Machine

After 40 years of seeming indifference, Florida has reopened its investigation into the murder of Harry T. Moore, the leader of the N.A.A.C.P. in Florida, and his wife, Harriette. But how sincere is the state about solving a crime that could expose a joint venture between Klansmen and lawmen, including a helping hand from the F.B.I.?

The Moore case is now being re-investigated on the order of Governor Lawton Chiles. And, while he is to be commended, the Governor was not prompted by a sudden impulse to right an ancient wrong. It came about because a brave Florida woman had revealed, in September, that her ex-husband, a Floridian now in his 70's, frequently boasted that he had been involved in the Moore killings.

Initially, one agent of the Florida Department of Law Enforcement was assigned to the case in September, but after demands by civil rights groups, four inspectors were assigned to the case.

New evidence was not the only reason the Moore investigation was re-opened. The "old" evidence is still brand new since uncensored information gathered by the F.B.I. had never been acted on -- though it had been in Florida's possession since 1980.

Indeed, the only material released on the case came from the F.B.I. in response to a reporter's Freedom of Information Act request in 1985. Even then, only 1,000 pages were made available -- with all but an estimated 3 percent of the contents blacked out.

The F.B.I. admitted that a remaining 1,923 pages were being withheld and that 30 pages had been destroyed. The reason? Protection of privacy, the bureau's inner workings and, unbelievably, "national security."

But even this minuscule offering provided frightening examples of what the lily-white F.B.I. and J. Edgar Hoover did, ostensibly to find the killers.

The bureau hired informants to record the license plate numbers of the 600 people who attended the Moores' funeral and then investigated all those who attended.

An F.B.I. agent reported that "it had to be a Negro who did the job, as no one else would know exactly where the Moores' bed was located." A subsequent report stated that the N.A.A.C.P. was also "definite suspect" in the killing and that "propaganda" and fund-raising purposes may have been behind the bombing."

All of these statements were absurd. There was not any evidence that remotely pointed in any of these directions. And the Klan had a floor plan of the Moore home which they shared amongst each other at Klan meetings. The F.B.I. agent stating that only a 'Negro' could know where the bedroom was in the Moore home was another absurdity, and a lie.

"They (the FBI) didn't stop there. The F.B.I. urged the Justice Department to appoint a particular judge, George W. Whitehurst, to preside over the Federal grand jury. They also urged the department to appoint as prosecutor James L. Guilmartin, "a Florida native who understands these matters."

Stetson Kennedy

2004
FDLE INVESTIGATION

The 2004 Florida Attorney General's Office of Civil Rights Investigation

Charlie Crist is an American attorney and politician who is currently the U.S. Representative for Florida's 13 Congressional District. He served as Attorney General from 2003 to 2007, after that becoming the 44th Governor of Florida from 2007 until 2011.

In 2002, when Charlie Crist was elected as Attorney General, he received support for his candidacy from the host of the television series, "America's Most Wanted", John Walsh. Walsh and other supporters of Crist endorsed him for his work with the Center for Missing and Exploited Children and for his strong agenda on crime.

Congressman Crist was also praised by civil rights and consumer groups for expanding the powers of the Attorney General, during his time in office. These powers would allow future Attorneys General to have greater powers, notably when prosecuting civil rights and fraud cases.

He was in favor of capital punishment and passed legislation requiring inmates to serve a minimum of eighty-five percent of their sentences before becoming eligible for parole. And As Chairman of the Senate Ethics & Elections Committee, he successfully investigated illegal actions of then-governor Lawton Chiles.

Charlie Crist was, indeed, tough on crime, and he was aware that the Harry and Harriette Moore murders had hung, shamefully, over Florida's head for decades.

The Moores' only surviving daughter, Evangeline Moore, met with and then encouraged Crist to try to locate or at least identify her parents' killers. Thereafter, an exhaustive investigation over twenty months employing thousands of man-hours and law enforcement resources sought to find the truth.

In 2004, Florida Attorney General Charlie Crist announced that his office was reopening the investigation to review the history of the case and seek any new witnesses or information that could lead to identifying those individuals responsible for the bombing.

On December 21, 2004, then-Attorney General Charlie Crist announced that the Moore case was to be reopened and investigated through the Attorney General's Office of Civil Rights. That Charlie Crist was able to muster government agencies to provide the enormous resources necessary to investigate a fifty-six-year-old criminal case was extraordinary, given the state of race relations in America. But Charlie Crist has a reputation best reflected in a saying by which he comports himself. He often says 'people over politics' And he is also known as a staunch defender of civil rights. Re-opening this controversial case was, for all intents and purposes, a good fit for Charlie Crist's ideology.

The purpose for reviewing the Harry and Harriette Moore case and subsequent investigations was to find new witnesses, study earlier evidence, and examine information more closely with hope to, once and for all, determine the identity of those responsible. Harry and Harriette Moore deserved some measure of justice. It was time for answers.

THE INVESTIGATION

The Attorney General's Office of Civil Rights interviewed over 100 persons over a 20-month investigative period and conducted a complete excavation of the sit of the Moore's home.

Attorneys and investigators for the Attorney General's office re-interviewed many of the people initially interviewed by the FBI, as well as other parties not questioned at the time of the bombing.

The Attorney General's investigation was extensive and concluded that Brooklyn, Belvin, Cox, and Spivey were likely most directly responsible for the bombing.

According to my conversation with the Florida Department of Law Enforcement (FDLE), Special Agent Dennis Nordell, who investigated the case for two years under then-Attorney General Charlie Crist, his observation was that other parties who were associated with the KKK definitely had varying degrees of involvement in the bombing.

But he also reiterated, due to the time frame and because of the locale where the bombing took place, it was unrealistic to expect to confirm the array of parties involved in the crime.

Certain witnesses and associated persons had been afraid to speak to law enforcement when the crime occurred. Former Special Agent Dennis Nordell indicated that many were still scared and had been threatened again (present tense), even though more than fifty years had passed.

Attorney General Investigator Frank Beisler and FDLE Special Agent Dennis Norred discovered that the Moore property where the bombing occurred had never been excavated by the FBI after the bombing. FBI conducted a crime scene search in the area and removed items of interest from in and around the explosive crater but did not professionally excavate the location.

Under Attorney General Charlie Crist and Allison Bethel (Director of the Civil Rights Office) Nordell and Beisler received approval to employ a professional archaeologist to excavate the property in 2004. They were hoping to locate artifacts that might allow them to identify what type of explosive had been used in 1951. Florida law mandated the recording of sales of dynamite; however, it was discovered that these records were rarely ever kept.

Also, Office of Civil Rights Director, Allison Bethel, requested that the FBI forward any information concerning bombings in the Miami area during the Florida Terror serial bombing era. The request was made to assist Beisler and Norred in determining if there were any similarities between the Miami area bombings and the Moore bombing.

Beisler and Norred traveled to FBI Headquarters in Washington to review files from 1951. They examined 17 original files and obtained copies.

Alarmingly, Nordell and Beisler discovered that crime scene physical evidence amassed by the FBI had long ago been destroyed or misplaced when it was handed over to the Brevard County Sheriff's Office (BCSO). They also noted that there were specific FBI files and original physical evidence accumulated by the FBI which had been destroyed after being tested in the FBI labs.

This evidence was never located.

Beisler and Nordell eventually developed a scaled-down list of suspects and began to concentrate on the motive and opportunity of these individuals to commute the murders.

The suspect list dwindled to 3 individuals. Joseph Neville Cox, Earl Jackson Brooklyn, and Tillman Holly Belvin, all Klansmen from the Winter Garden and Orlando Klaverns who had violent reputations. These investigations revealed a fourth suspect, Edward Lee Spivey who held the position of Exalted Cyclops in the Orlando Klavern.

It also appears that members of the Orange County and Apopka Klan Klaverns discussed the bombing and may have provided supportive assistance to the perps. FBI records also indicate that the perps once the explosive device was detonated, left Mims and went to the "Fagan's Marina Lounge" in Ft. Pierce to meet with other Klansmen to celebrate the bombing.

Beisler and Norred determined through the assessment of evidence and interviews and documentation that the bombing of the Moore's was likely carried out by a small group of renegade Klansmen who possibly acted without official consent of the Klan.

In other words, although the bombing incident was discussed at Klan meetings, it appears that the Klan, per se, did not officially sanction this action.

Norred and Beisler revisited the Groveland case. From FBI files showing the shooting scene of Irvin and Shepherd. They noticed something significant. Sheriff McCall had stated that he had a flat tire on the left front of his vehicle when he pulled over and shot his two prisoners. But there was no flat tire.

However, FBI still exonerated him saying physical evidence confirmed story that the defendants attacked him. Nordell found records confirming that McCall's Deputy Sheriff Yates falsified evidence to get a conviction on the Groveland case. The plaster footprints were falsified and the evidence of same was never admitted in court.

Evangeline Moore surmised that her parents were killed on orders from state government and perhaps former KKK member Governor Fuller Warren.

Nordell says: This investigation does not in any way conclude that only the individuals named in this case were the possible perpetrators involved

Charlie Crist and Juanita Evangeline Moore

in the conspiracy, planning, preparation and execution of the premeditated murders of Harry T. Moore and his wife.

It is firmly believed that there is a probability of other individuals being involved that were not uncovered by this investigation primarily due to the passage of time, lost, misplaced, destroyed, or hidden information and evidence, and people being afraid to come forward, including current members of the KKK. Even today, those who are alive fear retaliation and reprisals for testimony they might provide to law enforcement.

Forensics teams combed the former site of the Moores' house for evidence, and hundreds of interviews were conducted in pursuit of results. No stone went unturned to find evidence, or as much as could be found, given the amount of time that had past.

But Attorney General Crist had an interesting perspective by then. He did not know if there would be any result from the investigation. But he also felt that not enough had been done to investigate the case. There were apparent omissions and errors, and he hoped that applying maximum effort would show good faith to the residents of Florida that 'the system' cared and was willing to step up to prove the black community that justice would be pursued with vigor and integrity.

There had been three prior investigations in the past and under Charlie Crist's instructions, all three were reviewed thoroughly in conjunction with his office's investigation.

This investigation truly was a comprehensive review and included an examination of the information gathered in prior investigations, a quest for knowledge, interviews, and a professional excavation of the bomb site.

Crist's team finally interviewed witnesses, gathered physical evidence, compiled reports and followed investigative leads, wherever possible. Some of the team's research also focused on the serial bombings (Florida Terror) which commenced approximately six months before the Moore bombing and continued for over six months after.

During the investigation, agents interviewed Klan members concerning these incidents to gain information on the Moore bombing. FBI had charged some of the Klansmen with perjury, and those proceedings were extensively reviewed to gather background, potential witnesses for examination, and investigative leads. Although the FBI's investigation was extensive, the Attorney General's team located and interviewed area residents and suspected Klan members who had not been previously interviewed.

The team also examined other civil rights cases which had been re-opened in recent years. In some of those cases, the perpetrators were identified with available data from the initial investigation but were suppressed or ignored at the time. In other cases, there were additional witness statements or analyses of physical evidence which had not afforded full attention.

Four persons were named as being responsible for the bombing. There were more persons of interest connected in different ways, before, during, and after the fact.

The four subjects who were named were ranking members in the Klan in the central region of Florida in the 1940's and 50's -- and they were persons of interest from the very first investigation in 1951-52.

Outside investigation by parties, not affiliated with law enforcement (authors, journalists, activists, NAACP members), who also studied the Moore case, agree, in part, that naming only Earl Brooklyn, Tillman Belvin, Joseph Cox, and Edward Spivey would be inaccurate. All parties believed others were involved in one way or another.

Unfortunately, the FDLE was unable to accumulate sufficient evidence to name other persons who were likely to have been involved. The local environment (Mims, in Central Florida) at the time of the bombing was rife with racism, politics, fear, mistrust, corrupt law enforcement, corrupt government officials, and aggressive white supremacist groups (KKK).

In reality, it was unlikely in the 2004 investigation that enough verifiable evidence could ever have been secured to indict or even identify all of those involved, given the less than ideal, circumstances of the time, the era, the science, the infrastructure, the parties involved, and location of the crime.

All four suspects were deceased.

We are all indebted to Harry and Harriette Moore for having the courage to speak out for justice. They paid the ultimate price, but their sacrifice was most assuredly not in vain. In 1958, a Senate investigative committee convened to hear testimony on evidence about the Klan that had been gathered in the Moore and other investigations.

Among those who testified was paid undercover informant Richard Ashe, who said Brooklyn told him he was involved in the bombings. Many arrests were made following the 1958 hearings and the Klan lost momentum and support. However, with today's internet and other organizational tools, the number of hate groups in Florida and the nation is on the rise.

Charlie Crist stated: *"We recognize that it is difficult to investigate a 50-year-old case, particularly one as complex as this. However, given the Moores' remarkable courage and exceptional contributions to the struggle against segregation, a final attempt to find the truth was undoubtedly justified. Other states that have attempted to solve old civil rights cases have found that the effort, regardless of its ultimate success, has helped heal some of the wounds caused by the racism of the past. It is hoped that this final chapter in the mystery surrounding the deaths of Harry and Harriette Moore will bring some measure of comfort and closure to Evangeline Moore and all Floridians who have sought justice for so long."*

Congressman Charlie Crist

CONGRESSMAN CHARLIE CRIST INTERVIEW
The following interview took place in
St. Petersburg, Florida on August 29th, 2017.

GREGORY MARQUETTE: I'm speaking today with Congressman Charlie Crist. Welcome.

CONGRESSMAN CRIST: Thank you.

GREGORY MARQUETTE: The journey that was yours and theirs (The Moores) was a long process of investigation. When did you first learn of the Harry and Harriet Moore assassinations?

CONGRESSMAN CRIST: I don't remember exactly when I first heard about the case involving Harry and Harriet Moore but it probably was early on in the timeframe that I had been elected Attorney General. Obviously when you get elected to a position such as that that deals with justice and issues of fundamental fairness, things like that come to your attention. I suppose it was probably the beginning of the term of attorney general.

GREGORY MARQUETTE: You raise a good point. In your own perception, being a Floridian your whole life, do you think the public or law enforcement or the public knew much about this case prior to your becoming attorney general? Was it common knowledge or was this something that lay dormant for a very long time?

CONGRESSMAN CRIST: I think it was the kind of thing that was not discussed very much at all. Having not heard about it earlier in my life is evidence to that fact, I think, which is sad because the work that he did in particular, Harry Moore, in civil rights, with the NAACP, civil justice if you will, were remarkable. He's a pioneer and should be remembered as such. Now I think he will be and her.

GREGORY MARQUETTE: Why do you think it was so quiet?

CONGRESSMAN CRIST: That's a great question. I don't know why it was so quiet or so little known. Maybe that's the way things were, and things of that nature, getting more civil justice done in our society was not something that was paramount in the South at the time. We're going back to the 50s and the 60s after all, and we've been through a lot in this country more recently, as we all know now in Charlottesville. Those aren't some of our proudest moments that we have some of those scars from the past in American history. Maybe a lot of people didn't want to remember it, but in order to not repeat things like that hopefully, it's important to remember and to never forget.

GREGORY MARQUETTE: Relating to the Harry and Harriet Moore killings, predating that only by a year or two, was the Groveland Four case, also an incredible story of racial injustice and judicial malfeasance, if I may say. How do you assess that relative to today when we look at this kind of a case and then look at today? Is there a parallel? Have we learned anything?

CONGRESSMAN CRIST: I think there are definite parallels between what happened to Harry and Harriet Moore in their murder and what's happening today with violence in Charlottesville, Virginia and other places, and it's saddening. To have us in the year 2017 and still having things take place that are reminiscent of what happened in the 50s and the 60s in America breaks your heart. I mean, it should. The rise of the KKK, of white supremacy, things of that nature, I never thought I would live to see something like that again, but here we are. It's a great tragedy, but I know we're a better country. I'm an optimist, and I know we're a better country. I believe that we can move beyond this and will. I look forward to that day.

GREGORY MARQUETTE: What was your feeling when you reopened the Moore case? How did you come to the point where you said, "I'm going to reopen a 53 year old case?

CONGRESSMAN CRIST: Somebody brought it to my attention. That's usually the way it happens in the attorney general's office. Somebody will come to the office and express the fact that there's this case, it's 50-some years old. No clear resolution has ever occurred in the Harry and Harriet Moore case and their death. The more you hear about something like that, if you have a heart for justice, then it's hard not to want to try to resolve it. The facts of the case are so tragic in and of themselves that a bomb would be set beneath their bedroom, that they would be blown up on Christmas evening, which also happened to be their 25th wedding anniversary. This should've been a time of great celebration, of great joy, of great happiness, and it turned out to be a tragic, horrific evening, resulting in their death.

GREGORY MARQUETTE: When you look back at 2004, I believe is when you reopened the case ...

CONGRESSMAN CRIST: Yes sir.

GREGORY MARQUETTE:: ...don't you feel that it is political, to some extent, to open a case that was that old, and have only the hope that you could find answers? It was bold. Did you feel that you could solve the case or was looking into the case sufficient, if only to show the effort?

CONGRESSMAN CRIST: My sense at the time was that a horrible injustice had been done. At a minimum, trying to find resolution of that injustice was paramount. Did I know we would be able to bring resolution to it? Of course not, but I knew it was worth the effort. At least in my heart that's how I felt, and that's why I did it.

GREGORY MARQUETTE: Pardon me but I don't know the structure. Is there pushback when you say, "I'm going to spend x millions of dollars, spend x hundred if not thousands of hours of research and resources," isn't there a pushback or an eye put on this that could be uncomfortable?

CONGRESSMAN CRIST: I don't think there's any question about it. There's always pushback whenever you're utilizing funds of the Office to try to pursue something, especially something as old at this case was. I don't recall it being that strong. Frankly, I think people would've been embarrassed to say that, trying to resolve an injustice such of this nature. We didn't hear a whole lot of that. There may have been more that felt that way that didn't want to express it.

GREGORY MARQUETTE: To be clear, it was only after becoming Attorney General that you even became aware of this case. Is that correct?

CONGRESSMAN CRIST: I may have heard a little bit about it in my prior role as Commissioner of Education for Florida. These were teachers after all and worked hard for education, public education on the East Coast of Florida, so there may have been some awareness. You're right, but it really didn't become front and center to me until after I had become attorney general in 2002.

GREGORY MARQUETTE: In my research, I discovered that other cases in other states had become 'a cause' to them, in a sense. Many cases were never solved, but in my investigation it showed that even the effort shown to the public that they were investigating had a positive effect, particularly in racial cases like this. Is this your impression, as well?

CONGRESSMAN CRIST: That was my experience that it did have great cause and effect and was appreciated, certainly by the minority community in the state and others, fortunately. Whenever you're trying to pursue the truth or trying to pursue justice, that's a good thing. We should never become a society that's stops doing that.

GREGORY MARQUETTE: Was it your experience or your investigators' or your team's experience that people were dubious or suspicious of this investigation, thinking, "Oh, this is a cosmetic effect. They don't really mean it," or "This is not something that is ever going to amount to anything"? Did you find people were cooperative or were they resistant or enthusiastic? What kind of effect did it have during the process?

CONGRESSMAN CRIST: My experience during the course of the investigation was that people were generally cooperative and took it seriously, fortunately. I'm sure there were skeptics. There always are. You're in a political environment. That's inevitable, but by and large, it was pretty well taken.

GREGORY MARQUETTE: Looking at this, would you say this case was important specific to Florida? I know that nationally we look at racism and injustice of all kinds in many ways, but particularly in Florida, and many people seemed to feel there was a black cloud hanging over Florida relative to this case not having been pursued... Was that something that you considered?

CONGRESSMAN CRIST: No, not really. I didn't think of it in just a Florida way. I thought of it in terms of justice being done and trying to reach a just conclusion. You think about the family members for example, the daughter and what suffering that must have brought on and not knowing who was responsible for what happened to her parents. I can't imagine living like that.

GREGORY MARQUETTE: What kind of resources were utilized to investigate this case?

CONGRESSMAN CRIST: The people within the Attorney General's Office - God bless them - we had about 400 attorneys. This was brought about in the Civil Rights Division of our office. They were there anyway, working, and it seemed to me that a very good utilization of their time and the resources available to us in the Attorney General's Office was for this case, along with others, but this one was pretty important, not only because it hadn't been resolved, but because of the historical nature of it. The precedent of what had happened to Harry and Harriet Moore and that it did happen in Florida was a tragedy that can't help but bother you.

GREGORY MARQUETTE: These murders predated Medger Evers, predated Malcolm X and Martin Luther King. It really was a visceral, powerful response that the Moore murders predated these iconic civil rights figures and yet they seemed to be the first in an era of civil rights activism that had not existed before. How did you feel when you discovered this information?

CONGRESSMAN CRIST: Well exactly that way. It's odd that they had met such a tragic conclusion to their life, and yet not much was known about it nor much credit to their efforts during their life to try to seek civil justice for minorities and for educators, frankly, until more time had passed. Others seemed to be credited with being more of the pioneers when these people (the Moores) really were.

GREGORY MARQUETTE: In my study of newspaper articles from Harry Moore's interviews around the time of the Groveland case, he filed a lawsuit against the board of education at one point because of the lack of pay parity for teachers. And he said something, which was fascinating. "They're probably going to take my life early," he had said many times. "I don't think I'm going to be around for very long because at some point, the hatred, the racial prejudices are going to take my life sooner than later, but it's worth it."

CONGRESSMAN CRIST: It's unbelievable that he would have that kind of clarity and actual thought process about the fact that the work he was doing may lead to his own demise earlier than it would have naturally and yet still wanted to pursue it, regardless. That's character, and that's courage, and that's remarkable.

GREGORY MARQUETTE: After the Groveland Four trial with Thurgood Marshall and its retrial, there was another interview in a Florida newspaper which said, "Don't you feel that you're at risk?" His comment was, "It's worth it. They may take my life early, but no matter what, it's worth it."

CONGRESSMAN CRIST: It's stunning courage. For him to say that what he was doing might lead to an early end to his own life and saying, "It's worth it to do that," how can you not honor and praise somebody like that?

GREGORY MARQUETTE: How long was the investigation?

CONGRESSMAN CRIST: About 20 months the investigation took us. I decided to move on it in December of '04 and not until the summer of '05 was it concluded.

GREGORY MARQUETTE: I saw an ABC television interview where you made the announcement. When you finally identified the four perpetrators who did you call first?

CONGRESSMAN CRIST: Who did I call first? It had to be their daughter (Evangeline Moore). I don't have a specific recollection of that conversation, but I'm sure it was her.

GREGORY MARQUETTE: Do you recall her response?

CONGRESSMAN CRIST: I recall her responses, ongoing. Sadly, she's not with us any longer either, but just a lovely person, who was very quiet and really didn't talk about it very much, but she was very grateful that there actually had been a conclusion reached about what happened to her dear mother and father.

GREGORY MARQUETTE: Then you announced it on television and to the general public. What was the overall response when you announced the results?

CONGRESSMAN CRIST: I think that generally people were pleased that a resolution had been able to be reached that the tragic deaths of these two civil rights pioneers could finally be laid at the feet of some people who actually perpetrated the crime.

GREGORY MARQUETTE: In the FBI report it states that the KKK supported the assassination process. The FBI was able to identify two KKK klaverns. Were they ever able to file charges against KKK members or were the four perpetrators the only ones officially named? Correct?

CONGRESSMAN CRIST: Right. It was strictly the four, and they were KKK members. Beyond that, it was limited to them.

GREGORY MARQUETTE: Two of the perpetrators died right after the Moore killings. Was it difficult to get the last surviving perpetrator? I believe he was still alive at the time you opened your investigation. Did he cooperate insofar as his giving confession or was this a process to get him to confess?

CONGRESSMAN CRIST: To the extent that I'm aware, he had given several confessions previous to different individuals, and people just weren't sure that those who actually were sharing that information directly what kind of credibility they had. From my understanding and recollection from the time, there was a level of cooperation that made it possible for us to reach a conclusion.

GREGORY MARQUETTE: Did you ever meet that person? Was he still alive at that time?

CONGRESSMAN CRIST: I did not meet him, no. The killers had some odd conclusions to their own lives. There was one who actually committed suicide after he had been interviewed by the FBI. I think his name was Cox if I remember right. Then two of them died almost exactly a year to the date after the bombings had occurred. It's eerie, but I think the daughter said herself that God has dealt with them in his way.

GREGORY MARQUETTE: The one that committed suicide, I understand in the FBI report he'd been interviewed a couple of times by FBI and they were closing in on him.

CONGRESSMAN CRIST: Right.

GREGORY MARQUETTE: I think the assessment or the understanding was that pressure and the guilt and fear weighed heavily, and that's why theoretically the suicide ... Is that your thought from what you knew?

CONGRESSMAN CRIST: That is my thought, yeah. Evidently, he had some kind of a mortgage challenge and allegedly was paid $5,000 to place the bomb under the Moore's home and was fearful, according to friends, that the FBI would be able to follow that mortgage and therefore be able to pin the crime on him.

GREGORY MARQUETTE: Track him?

CONGRESSMAN CRIST: Right.

GREGORY MARQUETTE: In today's world as we look at Virginia and other events recently whether it's Trayvon Martin or other cases, how do you feel about where America was then versus where we are now? What is your overall assessment?

GREGORY MARQUETTE: My assessment of race relations back then when these people were tragically murdered and where we are today is that we have a long way to go still. It saddens me to say that, but it's hard to reach any other conclusion, I think. When you see neo-Nazis, KKK, white supremacists not even hooding themselves, but showing their faces almost as if they're proud of it, is pretty stunning in this day and age that that is still going on and something is resurrecting it, and I don't know what it is.

GREGORY MARQUETTE: There are theories, discussions, analyses of the eras of 50s, 60s, 70s, versus today. The concept that the communications and social media has allowed a certain amplification of this negative behavior, and I suppose, in a way tacit, if not full support for each other.

GREGORY MARQUETTE: Right.

GREGORY MARQUETTE: Do you think that has some bearing on it?

CONGRESSMAN CRIST: I think that social media may have some bearing upon what we're seeing. In many ways, social media can be such a positive influence. Sadly, it can have the reverse effect as well. It looks like that is part of the problem.

GREGORY MARQUETTE: When you talked to Evangeline Moore, can you tell me what is the most memorable thing you remember from dealing with her vis-a-vis your journey to solve this case?

CONGRESSMAN CRIST: Her demeanor. She almost seemed holy. Such a kind, caring, forgiving soul. It really struck me.

GREGORY MARQUETTE: The governor at that time, was he Republican?

CONGRESSMAN CRIST: Yeah, Jeb Bush.

GREGORY MARQUETTE: Your political mandate is 'people before politics'. You are very much a supporter of civil rights. So on a political level, how was investigating this case perceived? How did you pull a racial case across the finish line? There had to be resistance on a political level.

CONGRESSMAN CRIST: Yes sir. Not the norm.

GREGORY MARQUETTE: Now you're a Democrat.

CONGRESSMAN CRIST: Happily. I feel at home now, finally.

GREGORY MARQUETTE: How did you find the wherewithal to jump in and say, "I'm going to do this"? Did you not get pushback or resistance?

CONGRESSMAN CRIST: There was pushback and resistance, particularly I think because I was the first Republican Attorney General in the history of Florida and yet brought this case, reopened this case if you will. I can only thank my parents for the upbringing they gave my three sisters and me and a sense of fairness and justice that they instilled in us, and that drove me much more powerfully than any allegiance to any political party or any pushback that one might receive. It's always been just part of who I am because of mom and dad.

GREGORY MARQUETTE: Speaking of that, then what was the gravitational pull for you to join the Republican Party based on what you just said? How did you end up going in that direction early on in your career?

CONGRESSMAN CRIST: Pretty simple. My mom and dad were Republicans, so I became a Republican. The Republican Party back then when I was an 18-year-old kid, you're talking just over 40 years ago, was quite different from what we're seeing today. It's moved so far to the right that I don't really recognize it. That's why I'm happy to be a Florida Democrat. A lot has changed, as well, but I was a Republican then for the same reason I was a Methodist. Because my parents were.

GREGORY MARQUETTE: Did you ever come to a conclusion as to why this case was unsolved, given your predecessors' investigations?

CONGRESSMAN CRIST: No definitive conclusion as to why it hadn't been resolved sooner. Theories, of course. Florida's in the South, at least the northern part of the state is, so there's that. Maybe there wasn't as much effort as you would have imagined or had hoped for to reach a conclusion because it was a dramatic case. To have a couple blown up in their own home, on their anniversary, on Christmas Day, you can't write that. It's a reality that's stunning in its drama, and to not have it resolved sooner than we were able to resolve it is sad.

GREGORY MARQUETTE: What jurisdiction did the FBI have in the 1950s in states? Were they not restricted or less respected or less known to states versus domestic law enforcement? Was this something they had jurisdiction with in Florida at that time?

CONGRESSMAN CRIST: I believe the FBI probably did. I'd have to research it to be certain, candidly, but my understanding of how the FBI works when local cases maybe are not being pursued, that's exactly the entrée for a federal FBI investigation to be initiated if for some reasons it's not being pursued on the local level in the way that it should.

GREGORY MARQUETTE: I understand people at that time in Florida were terrified if a police officer knocked on your door in that era. Many people, both in the judiciary and law enforcement, were sympathetic to racism points of view at that time. My take on this was that many people were nervous to cooperate, nervous to share information, nervous to come out and say anything to law enforcement. Am I correct?

CONGRESSMAN CRIST: Yes, and in fact, there was even some concern at the time and shortly after the actual incident occurred that some in local law enforcement may have been Klan members themselves.

GREGORY MARQUETTE: I understand there was a governor at one point that was a Klan member or at least involved in some extent with the Klan. I would think that this case could have made more progress had there not been that fear.

CONGRESSMAN CRIST: I don't think there is any question. When you think that elected officials, local law enforcement members, some of which probably were members of the Klan at the time, there would naturally be fear of bringing a case like this by a local state attorney or what have you.

GREGORY MARQUETTE: There were three investigations prior to yours.

CONGRESSMAN CRIST: Yes sir.

GREGORY MARQUETTE: There was the one right after the killings in 1951. There was another in the 1970s and one in the 1990s.

CONGRESSMAN CRIST: Right.

GREGORY MARQUETTE: In that process, it seemed like they were going over the same territory, and they tried however valiantly they did, they seemed to make some progress but never really got to the point. They had suspicions, as I read, particularly the third investigation. What was different about your investigation that was more successful than the prior investigations and ultimately solved the crime?

CONGRESSMAN CRIST: I think the difference in the investigations that were done in this case, four of them total, was the dedicated people in the Attorney General's Office that I had the honor of working with. They were truly dedicated to it in our Civil Rights Division and to pour over it for 20 months, to hire archeologists to excavate the grounds, which had not been done to that level before, it took a real dedication, and they deserve a lot of credit for their work.

GREGORY MARQUETTE: Would you say that some of the scientific advancements such as DNA and other scientific developments used in law enforcement today were key elements?

CONGRESSMAN CRIST: It's probably true that modern technology certainly helped. We had the opportunity to send a lot of the materials to Quantico, Virginia for testing that may not have been available back in the 50s, the 60s, or even in the early 90s.

GREGORY MARQUETTE: You had an enormous team of people operating in the investigation. How did you select your people?

CONGRESSMAN CRIST: Well you can certainly request help, and obviously we knew we were going to need all the help we could get for a case like this that nobody could resolve before. It did. It included FBI, Florida Department of Law Enforcement, obviously led by the Office of Attorney General, the chief legal officer of the state. Those forces all cooperating together brought us to the good conclusion that we were able to make and resolve.

GREGORY MARQUETTE: The amount of hours and resources and money, what did that cost? I know you probably don't have a final number, but it was a very expensive process. Twenty months of work. How many people were involved in the investigation?

CONGRESSMAN CRIST: Oh, literally hundreds of people were involved in the investigation. It takes tremendous resources to dedicate to a case like this, and for the length of time of the investigation, 20 months is not a short period. If your pursuit of justice is something that you think is important, not only to your state but your country and the people that you serve, that's what you do.

GREGORY MARQUETTE: I saw your announcement. I think it was ABC News with one, I think CBS did another, where you were on television saying, "We've identified the four perpetrators." It's certainly a strong Florida story, but I didn't see a lot of national media picking up on this. Does that surprise you?

CONGRESSMAN CRIST: Why national media wouldn't have focused on it more so, I can't answer that. I don't know what else was going on at the time for example. There may been a big hurricane somewhere, you don't know.

GREGORY MARQUETTE: It gets lost in the news cycle.

CONGRESSMAN CRIST: Sometimes it does.

GREGORY MARQUETTE: Congressman Crist, when I look at your investigation I look at it through a slightly different set of optics than...

CONGRESSMAN CRIST: Sure.

GREGORY MARQUETTE: ... some others might. I feel like this was brave to take on a case that you very likely weren't going to solve, or so it must have seemed, at first. Did you lose sleep over this?

CONGRESSMAN CRIST: No. I'm a pretty settled, calm person. No, I didn't lose sleep about it. I knew whatever the outcome was going to be was going to be, but I knew that it was worth the effort regardless.

GREGORY MARQUETTE: That's my point. You didn't worry about getting a final result; making a big announcement. You wanted to show, with purpose, that you were going to open this up and look at it in a magnified way. Would that be an accurate statement?

CONGRESSMAN CRIST: It would. And I think it sends a message that if you have people that are willing to use what's available through their office to pursue justice even if it's from a long time ago, maybe that can have a deterrent effect on somebody doing an injustice in the future.

GREGORY MARQUETTE: Other states I read about who did exactly what you did for other reasons, other cases, they reflect what you are saying. Many cases were not solved, but the overriding result or societal response was positive because, even if you didn't find an answer, you could show you were pursuing injustice. You were going after situations which were criminal or discriminatory behaviors. You could show a positive result just for the effort. That's what I'm asking.

CONGRESSMAN CRIST: Without a doubt. There's a positive result just by knowing that somebody cares and that these things will not be left to stand, that there is a rightness about what is being done. Candidly, the way that I've always looked at politics has not been right versus left, but rather right versus wrong and trying to right a wrong, which is exactly what we did in this case, I think is always important.

GREGORY MARQUETTE: If you had to put a name on it - moral victory?

CONGRESSMAN CRIST: Yes, I think it is a moral victory. I don't think there's any question about it. And certainly it was a victory for the daughter of these slain people.

GREGORY MARQUETTE: Did she (Evangeline Moore) hug you?

CONGRESSMAN CRIST: Yeah, she did. She did. She was very sweet.

GREGORY MARQUETTE: It must've been an emotional moment to look at her and talk about this. I'm asking on a personal level. How did you feel to finally get her in the room and say, "We did it"?

CONGRESSMAN CRIST: Well it was wonderful to actually see her in person and to be able to share the fact that this case had finally been resolved. Can you imagine? Your mother and father are murdered, and there's no resolution, no finality. To be able to reach that and be part of giving that to her. It was a great moment!

GREGORY MARQUETTE: Now that she's passed, recently, I would think that in your heart you feel a sense of, not only justice, but a sense of value for giving her that before she passed away -- a resolution, a resolve.

CONGRESSMAN CRIST: I hope so. I hope that for Evangeline it was a resolution that could have given her peace before she passed. I'm sure it did in some way.

∽

The 2004 investigation under Attorney General Charlie Crist was able to confirm the most 'likely' assassins of Harry and Harriette Moore.

Circumstantial evidence (after 53 years) pointed to four Klan member named Belvin, Brooklyn, Cox, and Spivey. And it was likely (though not able to be confirmed) that the Ku Klux Klan (KKK) did not directly sanction the bombing, but were aware of activities relating to the bombing.

The Attorney General's investigators indicate there were other persons involved and that the four named were likely the 'foot soldiers', and not the instigators. Special Agent Dennis Nordell clarifies this in his interview later in the book. He reiterates there is no hard evidence to confirm the assumption.

Congressman Crist indicates that he was pleased to have done it, no matter what the outcome.

Other states in America have attempted to solve historical civil rights cases and found that the effort, regardless of its ultimate success, had helped heal at least some of the wounds caused by violent racial incidents of the past.

"I can only thank my parents for the upbringing they gave my three sisters and me and a sense of fairness and justice that they instilled in us, and that drove me much more powerfully than any allegiance to any political party or any pushback that one might receive."

⌒ Congressman Charlie Crist

INTERVIEW WITH ALLISON BETHEL

Allison Bethel was born and raised in Chicago. She attended North-western University for undergrad and went to the University of Florida Law School after which she joined a prestigious Florida law firm. She joined the Attorney General's Office in 1996 under Attorney General Bob Butterworth. From 1996 to '98 she did eminent domain, and from 1998 to 2000 she became Assistant Director of Civil Rights. From 2000 to 2008 she was the Director of Civil rights for the Attorney General's Office.

ALLISON: When Charlie Crist was elected, I tell you, it was very interesting because I was a government lawyer, but I wasn't really very sophisticated in those areas. I remember meeting with his (Charlie Crist's) transition team and to be frank, Greg, I just sort of figured I was out.

GREGORY: Why is that?

ALLISON: I didn't have any connections. I was just this poor little black girl from the south side of Chicago, which is very democratic. I didn't even think I knew any Republicans until I met him, or if I did they were in the closets so to speak. I started my whole interview by saying, "I understand this is a new administration and a new time, and I'll be asked to leave. Hopefully, we can negotiate a professional separation." And they said, "Well wait a minute, maybe not. Tell us a little bit about the civil rights work you've been doing and what you'd like to do because Charlie Crist is very interested in civil rights." And I said, "Wow."

GREGORY: It surprised you?

ALLISON: It really shocked me. The antithesis of my experience that Republicans would be uninterested in civil rights, and this new guy and everything. I told him what we had done, and some things I'd like to do that were unfinished. They asked me to stay on and reappointed me. I was absolutely stunned. I had it in my mind I was ready to move on, and I never thought that a Republican, number one would be that interested in civil rights. And then to the extent that they were, I just figured they would have their own people. By then I knew politics was 'who you knew.' But I had gained some credibility in the African American legal community: 'street cred' maybe. I learned later that people who spoke on my behalf and said, "We know Allison. She's good. You'd be lucky to keep her."

GREGORY: What was your formal title at that point when you were working under Charlie Crist?

ALLISON: I was Director of Civil Rights for the Florida Attorney General's Office.

GREGORY: Did your responsibilities change under Attorney General Crist versus the prior administration?

ALLISON:: It didn't really, in that, that position enforces civil rights laws throughout the state of Florida on behalf of the State. The Office of Civil Rights is a statutorily created office. And there are some things that the office is supposed to do, but much of what is or is not done in that office is discretionary with the Attorney General. So, he or she can make it as aggressive as they want, depending on their philosophy.

GREGORY: You were pleased to be reappointed?

ALLISON: I was pleased, but I wondered if it was more or less a token. It turned out not to be. Charlie Crist, he's a great politician. I mean nobody's gonna' come in and abolish that office. But what they're going do is just diminish its significance in the broad scheme of things, and they can certainly do that in the law. I had spent these last few years under Mr. Butterworth, revamping the perception of that office and trying to move the needle forward. I really didn't want to be a token appointee. He (Charlie Crist) really wanted to do civil rights work. He shared ideas with me. He sought my counsel. He was interested in improving civil rights in Florida. These laws were a new strategy if you think of civil rights history. Early civil rights had the federal government working against the states in many ways and the main civil rights work had

been done by the federal government. It is this idea that a
state should be aggressive in civil rights and instead of just
deferring to the feds and waiting for the feds. This was a
pretty new concept that had begun under Butterworth and
was continuing under Crist. This was a learning experience
for me. We were able to get things passed after a couple
sessions due, in part, to Charlie Crist's aggressive pursuit of
it. And in some ways, it was received better from Charlie
Crist than it was from a liberal Democrat because when you
have a Republican saying 'let's do this', it took on a different
meaning.

GREGORY: Because when a Republican administration with a
Republican Attorney General comes along and says: let's do
X or Y, that would have an impact.

ALLISON: It most definitely would. The essence of Charlie Crist's
proposal was to expand authority for civil rights enforcement
by the State Attorney General in Florida and put that office on
par with the kind of authority the federal government has. So,
not only was it a Republican but here's a Republican asking for
an expansion of civil rights. I mean, who does that?

GREGORY: What was it that he was advocating?

ALLISON: We proposed a new provision that, based on the federal law,
where the federal Attorney General can address issues that
under two circumstances. One, where they raise an issue of
great public importance, and two where there is a pattern
and practice of discrimination. And if either of those two
situations occur the Attorney General may initiate action,
lawsuits and such. So, our proposal was that the Florida
State Attorney General should have that same authority
as the federal government to address issues of great public
importance or patterns and practice in Florida.

GREGORY: I said to Charlie Crist: "You're coming in as Attorney
General and then one day you announce you're going to
investigate the murders of Harry and Harriette Moore
assassinated in 1951. Did you know about this case prior to

becoming Attorney General?" He said, no. Is this true for you, as well?

ALLISON: Yes.

GREGORY: How is possible that something so important could have been so, shall we say, swept under the carpet, or marginalized?

ALLISON:: This was a disgrace in the history of Florida, but not any more so than the rest of the country. The murders of Harry and Harriette Moore were known, a little, in Mims, in the area where they grew up. But there are many areas of black history, in particular, the civil rights movement, that don't make it into the history books and are not talked about. This was one of them.

GREGORY: I've covered FBI documents, and in additional research in 1951, relative to the KKK's activities in the communities across Florida, and they indicate that there were 12 bombings that year in one particular area of Florida.

ALLISON: Yes.

GREGORY: Today, they would call that domestic terrorism.

ALLISON: Yes. Now we do.

GREGORY: What did law enforcement call it then?

ALLISON: SOP. (Standard operating procedure.)

GREGORY: 12 bombings in one year? It's remarkable.

ALLISON: Yes.

GREGORY: It appears that the FDLE (Florida Department of Law Enforcement and the FBI) that they attribute all 12 bombings to racial crimes committed by the KKK. But due to circumstances, the times, lack of manpower, lack of evidence, they could not prove it. Is this your understanding?

ALLISON: Yes. The KKK was very active then. They had a lot of visible as well as invisible support. And as the NAACP and people like Harry Moore and others were getting more active, the KKK acted just as terrorists do; they try to silence those who are making waves.

GREGORY: The word the KKK used to describe Harry T. Moore, according to FBI reports, was; "troublemaker."

ALLISON: Yes. Harry and Harriette Moore were definitely seeing progress and they (the KKK) were disturbed by it.

GREGORY: What kind of progress?

ALLISON: They increased membership substantially in the NAACP during those years. It went from a sort of outlier to gaining support within the black community. Florida was a sort of 'go along get along' state. Things weren't as bad, or so they felt, and so there were a lot of people who at first didn't want Harry riling things up; making waves. But, I think the iniquities were something he had to speak out on.

GREGORY: Newspaper articles quotes Harry many times: "Isn't what you're doing very dangerous?" And he replied each time: "Well I don't expect I'm gonna be here very long." More or less he said, "They're gonna take me out. They're gonna kill me before the day is done." He knew he was not long for this world the way he was operating.

ALLISON: The dangers in his work were not lost on his family. Mrs. Moore would talk about how they would all pray whenever he left for one of his meetings. His family never knew if he was going to come back or not. It's remarkable what they did in the face of these fears.

GREGORY: When were you first introduced to Harry and Harriett Moore?

ALLISON: I first learned about it from Charlie Crist. I got a phone call one day at my office. I really had not been involved in a criminal investigation. And I was surprised that he wanted to take it on, period. There were many who felt it was not a good idea because it would rile up too many people, and who knew what the outcome would be uncertain. But he was committed to it, in part, because of their daughter, Evangeline Moore.

GREGORY: She had a strong impact on him.

ALLISON::   Absolutely. He was touched by her story. She was a compelling woman; she that made him want to dig into this. The Office of Civil Rights for the Florida Attorney General's Office had never done anything like that before.

GREGORY: I asked Congressman Crist: "Isn't it a risk to take on a 57-year-old racial crime and not know the outcome? What if you didn't find the answers? What if you had nothing to report after all that time?" He told me it was 20 months of work, many hours, and a lot of money. He said he said that he would have done it anyway.

ALLISON: I believe that. He felt it needed to be done, it should be done, and let the chips fall where they may. I learned another remarkable thing about him. You cannot judge someone by their political affiliation.

GREGORY: His political by-line was: "People over politics."

ALLISON: Yes. A side story, one of the cases I handled under him, was a case where we were investigating an allegation of discrimination by the Lake County School against minority students and in connection with that I had to travel to Lake County. There came a time where I was going there and, I was going to meet with the Superintendent. I would report to Crist directly about what was going on in my case. So he knew I was having this meeting and he said, "Well, you know, I think I'll go to that meeting. I want to see this Superintendent myself and ask her why she is doing what she's doing." Comes time, to travel and he calls me and he says, "Where are you staying?" I told him where I was staying in a modest, budget hotel. And I gave him the name of nice hotel nearby where he could stay.

GREGORY: Best place in the area?

ALLISON: But he said, "No, I'm not gonna stay there. I'll stay where you're staying." I said, "What? Really? You're gonna stay at The Best Western?" Or whatever it was, and he said, "Yes." And I said, "Okay then. See you there. Maybe we can have dinner?" And we did. I just share that to say that I was surprised at how down to earth this man was, in terms of dealing with people, organizing his life, being Attorney General.

GREGORY: Did Charlie Crist trigger the FBI's and FDLE's involvement in the investigation?

ALLISON: Yes. We reached out to FDLE, the FBI, and local sheriffs. They were all helpful. They were terrific, FDLE particularly. FBI came to the table, too.

GREGORY: Did you coordinate the law enforcement activities?

ALLISON: Correct. We sat down with everyone and indicated that we planned to leave no stone unturned. We coordinated with FDLE, because they could get into places quickly. Dennis Norred and Frank Beisler were the foot soldiers. They did exhaustive interviews. And we met weekly, going over what we had, where this might lead us in terms of the next step, and just approached it in a strategic way. We tried to look at it with fresh eyes.

GREGORY: What kind of cooperation did you get?

ALLISON::   A lot of people weren't thrilled to talk to us, for a variety of reasons.

GREGORY: Why is that?

ALLISON: Some, in the black community still were a little skeptical about what Crist was doing. People of color distrust law enforcement and government. And whether their motives are true or not, and maybe some had something to hide, or were afraid.

GREGORY: Was it strictly focused on Harry and Harriett Moore, or did it include other related criminal incidents – like the 12 bombings – or the Groveland Four case?

ALLISON: The focus was the Moore's and to the extent that the Groveland Four and other incidents that Harry was part of, we looked at those with a view towards trying to find people who were still alive who may be able to shed some light on it.

GREGORY: The Groveland Four case was another heinous travesty of justice in that area of Florida with the sheriff, at that time, being Willis McCall. I found interviews and evidence which connects with Harry Moore. Harry was heavily involved with the NAACP at that point. There is evidence indicating certain persons from the Lake City area were members of the KKK and one, in particular, was a specialist with dynamite, which was the explosive used to murder Harry and Harriette Moore.

ALLISON: Right.

GREGORY: There was a connection, the FDLE suspects, and the FBI alluded to it as well, that Willis McCall was in some fashion, a party to, or aware of the pending bombing, though not an instigator necessarily, but possibly complicit in the Moore murders. They wanted Harry and Harriette Moore out of the picture. It is alluded to in the reports, but it could not be proven with so much time passed.

ALLISON: I think so. I remember. He (Sheriff McCall) was a mean dude. We looked at McCall. We looked at that case because that was one of his bigger cases. This is part of why Harry was so controversial, even within the black community. Nobody liked the way things were, but there was some comfort level, and blacks were afraid to rile things up. That Harry persisted in the face of that kind of opposition from the side that you're trying to help is remarkable. He was a visionary. I think he saw the greater good.

GREGORY   Dennis Nordell (FDLE) raised the point that as much as he focused on the crime, the division between black and white was very apparent. A lot of the black community were afraid of what Harry was doing, or they were not supportive of it. And he said what you just said, "Don't make waves; it's gonna make it worse."

ALLISON: I think we've made some gains, but we've become complacent. We do have more rights than we did then, but you only need to look at inequities in the schools, the criminal justice system. Law enforcement, housing, to see that there's just so much that remains to be done. And I feel certain this last couple of years has given voice to the bigots again in a way that we've not seen in awhile. People feel much more open to say we don't want blacks in our neighborhood. A lot of fear and hatred against immigrants. And I also see disturbing evidence of blatant discrimination taking as back to the days of Harry Moore - with these police videos and activities of how suspects are treated. I think we've lost ground.

GREGORY: How do you assess your experience working with then-Attorney General Charlie Crist?

ALLISON: I think we were fortunate in Florida when we had Attorney's General who were willing to act, and willing to act even before laws got passed and even to act when it might cost them some political capital with what the result is. Charlie Crist was courageous to take on the Harry and Harriette Moore case and other initiatives that he did because they were the right thing. Maybe some of these other folks (politicians) need to consider that. It was a career highlight. I didn't come from status or wealth. But growing up I saw the inequities in my neighborhood, and the neighborhoods of my other white friends, and to be able to work on these issues and bring my professional skills to it as well as my personal passion, was just wonderful. I'm so glad that he gave me the opportunity.

~

INTERVIEW WITH DENNIS NORDELL

Dennis Nordell was on the highway patrol in Florida starting in 1968. There was an attempt to make Florida a state police organization instead of solely highway patrol. The state wanted an investigative arm and so they created the old Florida Bureau of Investigation, which soon turned into the Florida Department of Law Enforcement. It operated directly under the governor and it became the investigative arm of the state for criminal investigations, either assigned by the governor or developed on their own. It became the state investigative arm of the State of Florida.

Nordell spent 26 1/2 years with the Florida Department of Law Enforcement (FDLE), 42 1/2 years altogether in law enforcement. He and his Special Agent partner Frank Beisler worked the Harry T. Moore investigation under the FDLE banner for then-Attorney General Charlie Crist. He retired in June of 2010.

GREGORY: I saw Charlie Crist's announcement naming the four people responsible for the bombing of Harry and Harriette Moore. But it appears to me that America, as a nation, knows nearly nothing about it.

DENNIS: You're right. They don't. They have no idea how important Harry Moore was. He was instrumental in registering everybody he could in the state of Florida, as far as black voters. I mean he 'busted his ass' big time.

GREGORY: It's not a well known national case, yet this case became a priority once Charlie Crist became Attorney General.

DENNIS: I was running all over the state back and forth doing other cases, as well, but we were very dedicated to this one because it was so important, historically, to make sure that we could get everything we could and make sure it was factual.

GREGORY: Why was it so important?

DENNIS: Because it set a precedent for what would happen later on. Even though Martin Luther King became the most prominent figure for black civil rights, he came long after people like Harry Moore. Martin Luther King didn't just rise to prominence. He had the communications, the technology of television, and community support. Harry had none of that. It was just Harry and his wife and two kids. And after they (Harry and Harriette) were murdered their two daughters carried on, to the extent they could. Evangeline Moore participated in so many ways. They (the Moores) were a well-respected family in that Florida community. And those girls (the two daughters) were fantastic.

GREGORY: At this time in history would you say this was a particularly difficult task?

DENNIS: They had to travel by rugged means. Harry Moore traveled around the state of Florida in a car to make personal contact with all the other chapters of the NAACP in Florida at that time and to register voters. He wasn't riding on horseback, but he was pretty close to having to ride on horseback everywhere he went. It was very hard for him to do what he did and he went all over the state, often on his own, often without compensation.

GREGORY: I read many newspaper articles where reporters asked Harry: "You know what you're doing is very dangerous? Do you feel your life is at risk?" he responded: "I know they're going to kill me eventually but I'm not going to stop." He knew he was a target.

DENNIS: This guy was dedicated, day and night, in trying to put together a plan and trying to support and make (voting rights and voter registration) popular, but trying to gather blacks together to have a united voice in the voting process. He really did, far beyond what he ever realized. After his house was bombed the trip to the hospital was a poignant event. It wasn't the ambulance that drove them to the hospital; it was a relative who drove him.

GREGORY: What were the police like with Harry Moore?

DENNIS: The police response was intermittent. We interviewed one of the police officers that went to the scene, and he said it was something that they knew was gonna' happen.

GREGORY: The bombing? The police knew?

DENNIS: They didn't know it factually, but they always felt, just by what Harry was doing. To them, he (Harry) was 'stirring the pot.' They felt something bad was gonna' happen to him or his family. It was well known that he was a target. A lot of people that we interviewed were (even at the time we did the investigation) in 2004, reluctant to talk about it.

GREGORY: Why is that?

DENNIS: People are still afraid of the Klan. The Klan, back during that day, and even on into the 1970's and 80's and 90's was strong and probably stronger in that part of the state than any other part in Florida, and even possibly stronger than other places in the United States. At FDLE we used to monitor Klan activities undercover and would we go to a lot of their meetings to videotape them. We identified participants and kept track of what they were doing.

                 So a lot of the people we interviewed, both black and white were reluctant to give us information and a lot of times they didn't want to meet us in any public places. They wanted to meet us in privacy - if at all. I remember one man, in particular, who didn't want to talk to us. He was a game warden who lived close to the Moore home. He was several miles away from where the Moores lived, but he heard the bombing the night they (the Moores) were killed. He was very reluctant to talk to us and tell us the whole story. I think he was actually a member of the Klan.

GREGORY: Even as recently as 2004 they were still worried about that?

DENNIS: Oh yeah, absolutely. Many of the blacks were afraid to talk to us and many of the whites, too. Like I say, we talked to not only him, but there was another guy towards the end of the investigation, we finally were able to run down, and I would bet a paycheck that he was a member of the Klan during the time of the bombing, and he lived close by to where Harry and Harriette lived.

GREGORY: When did you start, what years?

DENNIS: That's a good question. I want to say the end of 2004. It would have been about the time and I was assigned by my commissioner's office at the time to go meet with the Attorney General, and the Attorney General's representatives that were gonna' be involved in the investigation and that was with Frank Beisler (Special Agent with FDLE) and I.

GREGORY: Allison Bethel, Director of Civil Rights?

DENNIS: Right, I met with them in a conference room in Tampa. They came in and said, "Well, we got this investigation and da-da-da, and we would like you to be involved with it since you do homicides." So they said, "We would like to have this wrapped up in a couple of months," because the Attorney General was fixed to get into upcoming elections.
I said, "Well, it's obvious that you don't want me because this is gonna take, in my estimation, a year, not less than a year and possibly could roll on into two years." They said, "You've got to be kidding?" I said, "Absolutely not." I said, "If you're gonna do it and do it right, that's the way I'm gonna do it, but if you don't want to do it that way, then I'm out of here." They did it my way.

GREGORY: Congressman Charlie Crist stated it took approximately 22 months.

DENNIS: Correct. I mean every time we would make a step, we would find that there are 10 more steps to take, 10 different directions to go.

GREGORY: How many people do you think you interviewed?

DENNIS: Over 100.

We found the more we did, it became more important the more that we did because we were really finding out some very detailed information. Some of it was known, some of it was unknown. You have so many hurdles. It just took us a long time to finally get to an end.

GREGORY: Four people were named. But were there more involved?

DENNIS: I think it was probably 'a group decision' to do this.

GREGORY: A conspiracy?

DENNIS: 'You four are the badasses. Take care of this.' They were the so-called 'hit men.' Maybe even had done this before?

GREGORY: There were at least 12 separate bombings in Florida in 1951 and 52. All race related.

DENNIS: We found that out during the investigation because we brought it up all the time amongst ourselves: how many bombings there were - and if we could connect any of those people - because to me, just like in the military, specialists in every field. I think these four guys were 'the specialists' in doing what they did and with the other bombings that were so close together and in the state during that particular point in time. It was obvious that these guys could have been connected to a lot of these bombings.

GREGORY: But there was no evidence to connect them?

DENNIS: Part of the Klan MO, so to speak, was anytime that they had a gathering, they would call other Klan groups in Florida. These guys, if they wanted to do a special operation, they would call in other groups, sometimes being very specific, saying, "Hey, we want the Brevard County group," or "We want the Okeechobee group," or this, that, and the other, and they would come together to do whatever the operation they were focused on. It would not be unrealistic to think that these guys not only did this bombing but did other bombings - but that's speculation. We knew they operated that way.

GREGORY: You knew that how?

DENNIS: We knew it primarily from just the knowledge of the Klan and what they did all over the United States. Knowledge from education, educating yourself and what we were doing within FDLE about following them around because every time we went to Klan rally or Klan meeting, all during my law enforcement career, in which the first part of my law enforcement career was on the highway patrol, and if we had a Klan rally within our area, we made sure that we were there because of any trouble that might come about. We were well aware of Klan activities and their operations for quite a long time. Other law enforcement officers were following them around.

GREGORY: In today's world, in 2004, when you were doing your investigation, you state that people were reluctant and afraid to speak with you on the basis that they still feared the KKK?

DENNIS: A lot of people were skeptical of law enforcement because they knew if they talked to law enforcement other people would find out and it wouldn't take long for the word to get around that someone is snitching.

GREGORY: What would happen if they did?

DENNIS: More than likely, the Klan would pay you a visit or they would make it known to you that you didn't want to be visited. Sometimes a Klan member would go pay a visit, saying, "Hey, we know this, that, and the other. You don't need to do this anymore."

GREGORY: So that was the threaten?

DENNIS: Oh yeah, big time. Just like the mafia -

GREGORY:	- but I think of the Klan as being more from the past. You're saying it operates even today.
DENNIS:	It does. During my investigations, we were still going to the Klan rallies and maintaining intelligence on meetings. We still gathered intelligence on them until the day I left. It still goes on.
GREGORY:	In 2004 you were called to Tampa. You walk into a meeting with Allison Bethel, Director of the Civil Rights Office for then-Attorney General, Charlie Crist, and they tell you that you're to investigate a race crime from 1951. What did you think?
DENNIS:	Well, the FDLE does a lot of cold cases. We do cases that - we're garbage collectors. We do things that other agencies don't want to do; they can't do because of finances, or it's very intricate. They call us in when a case is very cold, and this one was more or less more frozen than cold. But it was still doable and that's what we looked at. We're still gonna have some people alive and we'll be able to talk to some. When I looked at the case I told Allison, "You're crazy if you think we can do something like this in three months. If you want to do it right," I said, "You tell whoever needs to know it, it's not gonna be less than a year and it's probably gonna be more like two years before we can ever get a handle on this and come to some type of determination." Regarding the bombing, you gotta' remember some people were mad about what Harry and Harriette were doing. White people, but they also had blacks were upset.
GREGORY:	Why?
DENNIS:	Harry was 'stirring the pot.' A lot of blacks didn't like it. If they were getting along in the community, they didn't want the pot stirred.
GREGORY:	You worked in cooperation with the FBI?
DENNIS:	We did receive cooperation from them. We were assigned an agent that brought us material, and it was interesting.

GREGORY:	Why?
DENNIS:	We had personal notes from J. Edgar Hoover. They had about 150 agents on it so they developed quite a bit of documentation. I mean this guy, Harry Moore, you know I can't put enough emphasis on what he and Harriette and his kids did. They were all involved in what their daddy was doing, and he was important as a figure in the black community, not only in Florida but throughout the United States for what was being accomplished. What he had to go through and all the hurdles he had to jump – these facts you can't wipe out.
GREGORY:	It sounds to me like you have grown, through your investigative process to admire and respect the family?
DENNIS:	There's no doubt about it. And their daughter, Evangeline, was 'a queen.' Harry and Harriette were very strong, well-educated disciplinarians and Evangeline was a wonderful person. Whenever we would find something (in our investigation), she would be the first person we would call to let her know.
GREGORY:	Tell me about Charlie Crist?
DENNIS:	He was a good Attorney General, just a good guy all around. I was proud he took this on because it could have blown up in his face.
GREGORY:	I asked Congressman Crist: "You had a five-decade-old case, what if the results were not productive?"
DENNIS:	It was very courageous because a lot of his people close to him tried to talk him out of it. "It could blow up in your face," some said. " You're involved in a lot of things; you may not want to stir that pot," talking about the Klan. Politically it wasn't something most politicians would do.
GREGORY:	He indicated that it was a cloud hanging over Florida and just felt it needed to be resolved one way or the other.

DENNIS: I can see him saying that. I can say, if you look back at his career in the Attorney General's Office, and not only that, but just basically in his lawyer career, he never backed away from anything that I can think of, and during his time as Attorney General, he got involved in some very touchy stuff.

Chapter 17
EIGHTEEN OBSERVATIONS

There are eighteen areas which, I believe, severely impacted the results of this investigation. I'm sure those who read this book or who know of this case may have their own insightful observations.

Here are mine:

1. J. Edgar Hoover ran this four year FBI investigation while harboring intense personal racial prejudice against African Americans.

2. Local Florida whites were uncooperative by virtue of their whiteness

3. Blacks feared violent retribution from whites and white law enforcement.

4. Local white population preferred to believe in false conspiracy theories or just didn't care who was responsible due to their racist pre-dispositions.

5. FBI investigators wasted precious time focusing on improbable suspects.

6. News media was entirely owned by wealthy white families and reported the news accordingly.

7. The Governor of Florida was a former active member the Ku Klux Klan.

8. The Governor's Special Investigator was a current active member of the Klan.

9. The crime scene was trampled at the Moore home contaminating evidence.

10. The FBI had no jurisdiction over murder cases in Florida.

11. Many whites dismissed Harry Moore as a troublemaker who brought it on himself.

12. Local residents and potential witnesses (black and white) were too frightened to speak with the FBI.

13. The Groveland case was a pinnacle of racist corruption and while a connection between that case and the assassination of the Moores was not proved, the events surrounding it and Harry T. Moore's challenging the system cannot help but lead one to believe there was criminal complicity.

14. Forensic science was not advanced sufficiently to provide adequate evidence.

15. Systemic bias, prejudice, and racism had infected government, law enforcement, judiciary since the creation of America. Proper cooperation and equitable justice was improbable, particularly in southern states.

16. An FBI spokesman allegedly stated (off the record) that things were best left alone so as not to "disturb the tranquility of the South", indicating at least this Special Agent's predisposition to 'not rocking the boat' or finding the killer(s).

17. Racism, prejudice, disrespect, and apathy permeated the FBI (at least to the extent that J. Edgar Hoover was guiding the investigatory process of a race crime).

18. Florida's law enforcement and legal system was corrupted by racism, bias, prejudice, cooperation and/or sympathies with the Ku Klux Klan.

Florida's history of lynchings and many thousands of racial injustices preceding the assassinations of the Moores, in Florida, (or anywhere in the South) was not a cooperative environment in which to investigate any racially-motivated hate crime.

And looking at 1950's statistics, history, economics, and logic, it was evident that the State of Florida and federal law enforcement were, indeed, incapable of delivering justice for crimes where African Americans or minorities were victims.

EMMETT LOUIS TILL

Only three and a half years after the Harry T. and Harriette V. Moore bombing a 14-year old African American boy, Emmett Till, was tortured and lynched on August 28th, 1955. There seemed to be no end to the race crimes in the South.

But this was considered to be one of the most savage slayings and scandalous injustices of this era, not only for the young lad's absurdly horrific murder, but for the outrageous injustice which allowed the murder charges to be dropped against these monstrous racist perpetrators.

Emmett Louis Till

Two whites named Milam and Bryant were charged and later acquitted by an all-white jury after only an hour's deliberation. This travesty of justice electrified the civil rights movement and instigated protests across America.

As of March, 2018, the Emmett Till case has been re-opened, based on the Department of Justice indicating they have acquired significant new information.

Emmett Till's death is a haunting reminder of the many racial injustices which African Americans still endure today.

Chapter 18

LIFE WITH HARRY MOORE

E vangeline Moore idolized her parents. They were shining examples of what parents and human beings ought to be. In December of 2003, she offered a speech about her father at a memorial service.

Evangeline Moore holding photos of her mother and father.

Speech: December 14, 2003
Harry T. and Harriette V. Moore Memorial Service
By Juanita Evangeline Moore

First Corinthians, chapter 13, verses 4-8 is my absolute favorite passage in the Bible. It reads "Love is patient, love is kind. It does not envy; it does not boast, it is not proud. It is not easily angered; it keeps no record of wrongs. Love does not delight in evil but rejoices with the truth. It always trusts, always hopes always perseveres. Love never fails."

Harry Moore was a loving person. He was the most patient person one could know. He was kind. He was never envious. He was never boastful. He knew no false pride. He was never rude. He was not self-seeking because he never bragged about what he was doing. He was not easily angered; I never saw him angry. He kept no records of wrongs. He was always forgiving. He did not delight in evil. He fought evil. He rejoiced with truth. He was truthful. He always trusted. He was trusting to a fault. He was full of hope. He hoped to make a better world for his people. Love never fails. He did not fail. Instead, he died.

First John, Chapter 3, verse 16 reads. "This is how we know what love is: Jesus Christ laid down his life for us, and we ought to lay down our lives for our brothers." Harry Moore laid down his life for his Black brothers, and he did it willingly.

My challenge to you today is "Strive to be a Harry Tyson Moore." To sum up, my description of Harry T. Moore's character I would say he was loving, had the strength of a Sampson and gave his all.

I have been asked to share with you what it was like living with Mr. Moore.

A day in the life of the Moore's. Breakfast, table set, we sit down to eat. Dad ate extremely slowly. We all sat at the table until he finished. Then off to school the four of us. When mom and dad taught at Mims Elementary School and Peaches and, I were in that school, we all traveled there together. We came back home to a quiet dinner. Dad took at least an hour to finish his dinner. We all sat at the table until he finished. Half way through the meal, one of us warmed the remainder of his dinner so that he would not eat cold food. He had a severe digestive problem.

Evenings found him in his rocking chair reading or at the typewriter typing. He was often the last to retire.

ENTERTAINMENT AT THE MOORES

On Saturday evenings we often played whist while listening to music. We had a graph-a-phone. The records were stacked in this order: dad liked blues and Negro spirituals. Mom enjoyed Hawaiian music, Peaches liked big band jazz, and I liked blues and anything that sounded romantic. My dad was a romantic person and I am still a hopeless romantic. Speaking of romanticism, my parents were a most romantic couple. Walking into a room and finding them embracing was commonplace.

There were other things we did for entertainment as a family always the four of us. We made many trips to the ocean on moonlight nights for picnics. Often on Saturdays, we drove to either Orlando or to Daytona to shop, have dinner and see a movie. The reason for our going such a long distance was that dad was determined we would avoid discriminatory practices in any form. Daytona and Orlando afforded Black restaurants and Black movie houses.

Dad was fond of Western books and movies. The first novel I read was "Drag Harlan" who had a very intelligent horse named Purgatory. I remember seeing Westerns like Jesse James and the Return of Frank James. I still look at re-runs of these movies whenever I see them listed in the TV guide.

MY PERSONAL RELATIONSHIP WITH DAD

I followed dad everywhere. I remember times when he was preparing to make his morning run to the Post Office and, I was not dressed. I'd call out "wait for me daddy." He waited, never impatiently. He was very protective. Peaches and I were not allowed to walk anywhere. I worked at Bethune-Cookman the summer after I graduated. My dad and mom had sublet an apartment approximately three blocks down what was then Second Avenue.

Dad drove me to work every morning; he was always waiting to take me home for lunch where mom always had a hot lunch waiting. He drove me back to work after lunch and was always waiting for me at the end of my workday. One of the most poignant memories happened the summer after my freshman year. Mom took classes at BCC and Peaches worked there that summer. I stayed home to prepare meals and run the household for my mother.

One night I awakened with one of my almost intolerable stomach aches. I had them often. Dad heard me pacing up and down in my room, came in and asked what was wrong. I told him my stomach was hurting. He left the room and came back with the hot tea my mother always gave me to ease the pain and make me drowsy enough to enable me to sleep. When I awakened the following morning, dad was asleep beside my bed in a rocking chair. How protected I felt!

Throughout my later childhood, through my teen's until I entered college, I was dad's girl Friday. I kept his papers organized; I ran the ditto machine - most of you don't know what machine was like. Xerox machines have replaced those machines. I stuffed envelops to be mailed, licked envelopes and stamps and, of course, followed him to the post office to mail them. In my early teen's I began delivering his yearly addresses to the NAACP State Conference Conventions. That meant months of my learning the material and his coaching me until my delivery was perfect. What nightmares I had about my delivery, but I never made a mistake.

The Florida State Conference of NAACP Youth Councils was very much alive. I was a state officer - either secretary and treasurer I believe. The president was Emmanuel Eaves from Jacksonville and the vice president, Henry Finley from West Palm Beach. Dad and I traveled frequently to those meetings. He was a brilliant historian, and we shared a love of poetry and prose. I hope my sharing "Life with Dad" with you has given you some idea of the great man he was. To me, he was just daddy.

I leave you with a statement he often used during meetings:

> *"Courage brother, do not stumble,*
> *though your path be dark as night.*
> *There's a star to guide the humble.*
> *Trust in God and do the right."*

INTERVIEW WITH LUCY SEIGLER

Lucy Seigler, a resident of Mims, was a close friend of Evangeline Moore. She attended high school with her and spent a good deal of time at the Moore home.

LUCY: I knew them from childhood because they went to school with me. He (Professor Moore) taught my sisters. I knew them because of their daughter, Evangeline.

GREGORY: When was that?

LUCY: I knew her since we started high school together in '47. We graduated from high school together. That was a little bit before the house was bombed. She was on the train coming home and wasn't aware that her parents had been bombed. Her uncle met her at the train station in Titusville. When she didn't see her parents, she asked her uncle, "Where are my dad and mom?" After a while, he spoke and said, "We have some unfortunate news to tell you, Evangeline. Your parents were bombed last night." You could imagine how she felt. She was shocked.

GREGORY: Did she have any sense of why it happened?

LUCY: I don't think she had any more knowledge than anyone else around here. Unfortunately, there are some people in the world just don't have the heart others have. People moved him to do what he does 'cause he was very smart and he wanted to help the community to get out and vote. That was his main objective.

GREGORY: He and she (Harriette) were very active in teaching people how to register.

LUCY: That's right. There's one thing about it, the community looked up to him because he was such a humble, kind person, and wanted to help people. It wasn't about hindering anybody; he wanted to help and make us aware of the fact that it's right to vote. Get out and vote, don't be lazy about anything, vote.

That's why we loved him so because he looked out for the whole community.

GREGORY: What were they like?

LUCY: They was just ordinary people just like my family was. They didn't try to be uppity, just on the same level. Ordinary people, I would call them. My parents allowed me to go every once in a while to see them, and if they wanted me to come and be with Evangeline. We played games that were educational games. They were just ordinary people that invited you into their home and loved you, and fed you if you need it if you was hungry.

GREGORY: Would you say that they were strong spiritually?

LUCY: Well, I know they loved the Lord and they did what my parents would do, say the grace before you eat. They honored God.

GREGORY: What was Harriette like?

LUCY: She was good. You couldn't have been around better people than they were, in my opinion.

GREGORY: It appeared that the Moores were targeted because of civil rights activities.

LUCY: Yeah, that would probably because I had heard about the KKK. All I can say is hatred is the key. It wasn't any love that was out. It was hate. When you're around hate, anybody that's hateful and have stony hearts like that, they'll do anything.

GREGORY: How did Evangeline react when she saw the Harry and Harriette Moore Memorial Center?

LUCY: She thought it was just beautiful to represent her father and mother like that, in that manner. They started putting bricks out there with names on it. She just thought it was wonderful.

GREGORY: What would you say about Harry and Harriette Moore to anybody who asked you?

LUCY: I would obviously let 'em know that Harriette and Harry T. Moore were wonderful people. When he was principal, he tried to get higher wages for the teachers. They weren't getting equal pay, and that's what he was fighting for. Equal pay for the blacks as well as the whites. Then that's when he, I guess the Lord showed him to get with the NAACP, and he could do more with a group of people like that. I just think they were just wonderful people. He worked for peace and love, and education.

GREGORY: What would you say about Harriette?

LUCY: The same thing, they worked together.

GREGORY: Harry Moore believed in freedom?

LUCY: I think it's on that same line because it's just like Martin Luther King, on the same order. When God gives you something and you're qualified to do it, and you can feel purpose in doing it, you don't care what people might do to you. Although, you might lose your life. Still, it's satisfaction in the work that they have done or are doing. That's why you can't stop, I guess. And Harry was a fighter, but not the way they thought.

GREGORY: He fought in a different way.

LUCY: He was fighting to help people in general. We learned a whole lot from Professor Moore. We still learn a lot from him. We stayed about three or four miles south of this area where I am now. When we would hear that Harry T Moore is gonna' talk with us about voting tonight, my parents made it their business to be to the church where he was gonna' be because they knew it was somebody who could tell the truth and really listen.

GREGORY: Did you ever see Harry give a speech?

LUCY: Mostly at the church - he was a good speaker. He just made things plain where we could understand what he was talking about. If there any questions, he wanted to hear it right then. And he was talking about NAACP and different things, yeah. It wasn't like speaking on TV, but it was a community thing because he could speak like a teacher.

GREGORY: Did you like his speeches?

LUCY: Every one of 'em.

GREGORY: Why?

LUCY: Because I knew that he was putting us on the right road. That's why whatever he said, we believed.

GREGORY: What else did he talk about, Lucy?

LUCY: I think mostly like how to share and love one another, or something of that nature. Just common things that our family should be teaching us anyway. He just was how important it is to stick together with one another.

GREGORY: Community.

LUCY: He really molded my life and whatever he said was very impressive to me as a young person.

Chapter 19
A FINAL WORD

Democracy is an amorphous structure subject to the will of the people and those chosen to represent them at any given time.

While most people are aware of white supremacist actions and mentality from watching a news broadcast, it should be noted from my research, and interactions with investigators, that these people operate today in much the same way prior supremacists had seventy years ago. Threats, intimidation, and violence were and are in their DNA.

During the FDLE and FBI's final investigations of the Moore case in 2004 and 2008, many witnesses were threatened if they offered testimony to law enforcement officials. They feared retaliation from Ku Klux Klan members or their associates. Eyewitnesses or parties connected to historical events would often avoid or withdraw from law enforcement interviews or offer to meet in secret.

While it is generally accepted that hatred and ignorance are passed from generation to generation, there is the hope that awareness and education may help to erode at least some of this, but how much is the question. The fabric of this country is undeniable. America's history is public record; victims are many.

As mentioned at the outset of this writing, 'history as prologue' must be given serious consideration and assessment, then vigorously addressed. We dare not repeat egregious errors made in the past. The costs are too high to imagine, and yet, history is being repeated on many levels.

While history provides a cautionary view, we can only hope that the fear of repeating mistakes will motivate some in society to take meaningful action to build a society where all men and women truly are created equal. These are fine words but not actually applied in today's society.

In the 1950's Harry T. Moore's activities inspired a wave of racist fury in the white supremacist world. In their view, this was not only an assassination of

Harry T. Moore and his wife, but it was also a message for those who would dare to challenge 'white authority.'

A black man was challenging them on a scale they had never seen before. His fearless confrontations of white authority made him a target and they, symbolically, chose Christmas Day to deliver their message.

Harry T. Moore was alone. But he could never stop. He knew action had to be taken for the sake of his race. No one in his part of the world was doing anything powerful enough to make people pay attention. So he challenged a savagely corrupt, white-run system, without fear, hesitation, restraint, or political correctness.

African Americans had suffered horrific treatment in America for centuries and, it was not about to change without serious action. He felt compelled to sacrifice himself by aggressively challenging the social, political, and legal systems which had accepted, supported, legalized, and endorsed savage treatments inflicted on African Americans.

In his view, it was time to do something.

Harry might not change America, but he believed he could make a change where he lived, and then hope to send his message to the rest of the country.

He defied the power system and made his voice heard. As we look back on his life, his words and actions, they resonate with America, even today. We must try to be better than we are. In his time, there was conspiracy on a grand scale; a conspiracy of apathy - of economics - of convenience - of racism. And there was a conspiracy of silence, motivated by fear.

The solace we may or may not take from this may only be that Harry T. Moore made a remarkable sacrifice to improve the quality of life for his race. For many, he offered and set an example of integrity, pride, confidence, courage, and belief in one's self. But this was more than many African Americans had, before crossing paths with the likes of Harry T. Moore.

Words are only words, but when we attach meaning and values to our words, supported by thoughtful actions, change is possible.

Harry T. Moore set an example for all of us.

From the many interviews I conducted, it was clear that the man was impressive. He offered his life to inspire others and to be brave to speak up for change. The fact that he has not been given as much credit as he deserves would probably not upset him. Harry T. Moore was not driven by ego or a need for attention. His pride would come from his knowledge that, in some way, he had an effect on his neighbors, on his community, on America.

Hopefully, more people will now be aware of and appreciate this man's life and the beautiful set of human values for which he stood and died. His contribution, whether we know it or not, made us all better than we are.

He was Harry T. Moore.

2008
THE FINAL INVESTIGATION

Updated March 20, 2017

JUSTICE.GOV
950 Pennsylvania Avenue, NW Washington, DC 20530-0001
U.S. Department of Justice - FBI "Cold Case Initiative"

In 2008, the FBI initiated a review of the bombing that killed Mr. and Mrs. Moore, pursuant to the Department of Justice "Cold Case Initiative" and the Emmett Till Unsolved Civil Rights Crime Act of 2007, Pub. L. No. 110-344, 122 Stat. 3934 (2007), which charges the Department of Justice to investigate violations of criminal civil rights statutes that occurred prior to 1970 and resulted in death.

The FBI reviewed the prior four (Harry T. Moore) investigations and files. The review of the previous investigations identified ten former members of the central Florida Ku Klux Klan who may have had pertinent information about the bombing. Further investigation involving interviews and research of death certificates revealed that eight of the potential witnesses were confirmed to be dead, and two were unable to be located but suspected to be dead.

An exhaustive review conducted by the FBI and attorneys from the Department of Justice Civil Rights Division did not produce any new leads.

Instead, the review suggests that the most probable subjects involved in the bombing were Brooklyn, Belvin, Cox, and Spivey. All four subjects are deceased.

To clearly understand the current FDLE and Florida Attorney General's Office Investigation and its results, it is important to fully understand the depth of the four prior investigations. These investigations form the basis upon which the current investigation is predicated. Summaries of those investigations are described in this report.

This Case Summary is not in any way meant to answer all of the questions concerning the events surrounding the December 25, 1951 bombing of the Moore family home and the subsequent homicides of Harry T. and Harriette V. Moore. Further, the Case Summary is not intended to purport or to indicate that the suspects developed during this investigation are the only persons involved.

This investigation and Case Summary, along with supporting documentation and testimony, clearly indicates that there are other individuals who were involved in the planning, intelligence gathering, conspiring and perpetration of the act and who were responsible for or played a significant role in the despicable act upon the Moore family.

LEGAL ANALYSIS

This matter does not constitute a prosecutable violation of federal criminal, civil rights statutes. First, despite extensive efforts, no living subject has been identified. All four of the identified primary subjects are deceased.

Second, even if a living subject could be identified, the statue of limitations has expired. Prior to 1994, federal criminal civil rights violations were not capital offenses, thereby subjecting them to a five-year statute of limitations. See 18 U.S.C. ' 3282(a). In 1994, some of these civil rights statutes, including 18 U.S.C. ' 242, were amended to provide the death penalty for violations resulting in death, thereby eliminating the statute of limitations. See 18 U.S.C. ' 3281 ("An indictment for any offense punishable by death may be found at any time without limitation."). However, the Ex Post Facto Clause prohibits the retroactive application of the 1994 increase in penalties and the resultant change in the statute of limitations to the detriment of criminal defendants. Stogner v. California, 539 U.S. 607, 611 (2003).

While the Civil Rights Division has used non-civil rights statutes to overcome the statute of limitations challenge in certain cases, such as those occurring on federal land and involving kidnapping resulting in death, the facts of the present case do not lend themselves to prosecution under other such statutes. Based on the foregoing, this matter lacks prosecutive merit and should be closed.

AUSA Carlos Perez, Middle District of Florida, concurs in this recommendation.

Available evidence, although not conclusive, links Belvin, Brooklyn, Cox and, to a lesser extent, Spivey, to the crimes. While the evidence is not conclusive, it is very strong. It is the opinion of those involved in this investigation that, were any of these suspects still alive, sufficient circumstantial evidence exists to present the case to a grand jury for possible indictments for the Moores' murders.

It is also possible that other members of the Klan, especially the Orlando and Apopka Klaverns, participated in the conspiracy to murder the Moores.

The record shows Moore and his activities were discussed at several Klan meetings and members were not pleased with Moore's growing success at changing the existing political structure. While the murders may not have been officially sanctioned by the Klan and the perpetrators were considered "renegades," other members of the Klan definitely knew Moore was being targeted.

It is also sadly evident that some members of area law enforcement were Klan members and/or sympathizers and may not have supported the FBI's investigation.

The damage caused by that regrettable state of affairs is still evident today, as this investigation concluded that a number of witnesses were reluctant to be completely candid with this investigation for fear of retribution.

Case closed.

Harry T. Moore is remembered for his dignity, his compassion, his discipline, and the great value he placed on education. He was a gentleman of learning, ethics, courage and persistence, and admired for his deep appreciation for the human values on which the founding fathers built America.

Highlights & Accomplishments

1934 — Organized and became president of the first Brevard County Branch of the NAACP

1937 — Organized a group who selected John Gilbert to file suit for equal pay for black and white teachers

1941 — Organized the first State conference of NAACP Chapters in the State of Florida

1941 — Became President of NAACP

1945 — Formed and became Executive Director of Progressive Voters League of Florida

1945 — Launched Voter Registration Drives in November increasing black voter state registration from 5% to an astonishing 37% with the slogan: "A Voteless Citizen is a Voiceless Citizen"

1946 — Brevard County School Board fires Mr. and Mrs. Moore over Moores' activism

1946 — NAACP names him State Executive Director

1948 — Moore demands State investigations of police violence against blacks.

1949 — Moore becomes the first African American to file a lawsuit against the School Board demanding equal pay parity between blacks and whites

1950 — Moore causes Brevard County to appoint first black deputy sheriff with authority to arrest both blacks and whites

1950 — Moore raises funds for the appeals of defendants Irvin and Shepherd in Groveland Case

1950 — Moore enlists NAACP lawyer Thurgood Marshall to defend Irvin and Shepherd

1950 — Moore's efforts aid in winning appeals for the Groveland defendants Irvin and Shepherd

1950 — The nonpartisan national NAACP objects to his sending out combined mailings to members of the NAACP and the partisan Progressive Voters League, signing his name and his titles in both organizations but Moore continues

1951 — Moore asks Governor Fuller Warren to remove Lake County Sheriff Willis McCall from office for shooting the two Groveland manacled black prisoners

1951 — Florida state NAACP convention, led by national officers, remove him as salaried Executive Director of the Florida NAACP, and made him the unpaid state coordinator; owing him nearly a year's back salary

ACKNOWLEDGMENTS

This book sprung from research done in preparation for the writing of a motion picture screenplay entitled The Unknowns—Talent Is Colorblind (referring to the unheralded artists from Florida known as "The Highwaymen"). They were a remarkable group of African-American fine artists who commenced their artworks in the late 1950's through the 1960's under the guidance and tutelage of a brilliant young man named Alfred (Freddie) Hair, who lived, painted, and passed in Fort Pierce, Florida. There are a number of Highwaymen still painting today.

It was during my research on this screenplay that I learned of the assassinations of activists Harry and Harriette Moore in 1951. The murders of Harry and Harriette Moore were committed in an era of extreme racism, ignorance, fear, denial and violence. And this racial crime spoke to the era in a way which reflected the actual tone and manner of America for anyone of color.

While The Unknowns motion picture introduces us to the era in which blacks in America had to endure extreme social injustice and racism — *The Bomb Heard Around the World* magnifies it in startling detail.

Fifty-three years later, in 2004, then Florida Attorney General Charlie Crist took on this unsolved case. Twenty months later he and his team finally identified the assassins of Harry and Harriette Moore. And in 2017, the Congress in Florida finally apologized for the miscarriages of justice imposed on the four young men who had been falsely charged with rape and who were either murdered, tortured, or imprisoned unjustly in the Groveland Four case.

Special thanks to CNN, United Press International (UPI), Associated Press (AP), the Miami Herald, Ebony Magazine, Southern Poverty Law Center (SPLC), The Smithsonian, National Association for the Advancement of Colored People (NAACP), Florida Department of Law Enforcement (FDLE), and the Federal Bureau of Investigation (FBI) for all photographs and published articles offered in this presentation.

Acknowledgments are also offered here to Alfred (Freddie) Hair and all "The Highwaymen" artists then and now, plus Zora Neale Hurston and Albert "Bean" Backus for their remarkable creative works and conspicuous inspirations which will live forever.

Special thanks to the memory of the very special Florida schoolteacher, Zenobia Bracy Jefferson, who brought this story to light.

We, at TOP CAT II PRODUCTION PUBLISHING GROUP, LLC, wish to extend our heartfelt thanks for all the time, effort and dedication the members of the Harry T. & Harriette V. Moore Memorial Park & Museum have given toward the research and creation of this book.   It was truly a pleasure to meet all of you and learn about the hard work and belief the Moore family carried in their souls; reflecting an unselfish effort to help those in the community find a better life.

SPECIAL ACKNOWLEDGEMENTS

Thanks to Walter T. Shaw for his tenacity with regard to this material and my heartfelt appreciation for his energy and creative vision.

Further appreciation goes to artist Lauren Garza for his remarkable artwork on the book cover and poster and for other fine works he has designed in the past.

Thank you to Gail L. Kaiser for hard work, professionalism, and excellent advice in the formatting of this book. Her guidance and contributions were invaluable and most appreciated.

Additional thanks go to Brian Bayerl (Director of Photography), Mark Weber (Sound Specialist), and Jeffrey Bloom, Esq. (Attorney at Law).

There are two special acknowledgements to be mentioned here. Congressman Charlie Crist deserves respect and praise for his tenacity and integrity in reopening the case of the assassinations of Harry and Harriette Moore. His strength of purpose and vision are to be commended.

A special acknowledgement goes to the memories of Harry and Harriette Moore and their two daughters, Juanita Evangeline Moore and Annie Rosalea Moore - also, to Juanita Evangeline's son Drapher ("Skip") Pagan Jr., grandson of Darren A. Pagan, and all members of the Moore family living and passed.

A SPECIAL THANK YOU TO:

MLF Michael L. Feinstein, P.A.
ATTORNEYS AND COUNSELORS AT LAW
Michael L. Feinstein, Esquire
ATTORNEY AT LAW

Malloy & Malloy, P.L. Patent, Trademark & Copyright Law

FROM THE PUBLISHER

The publisher wishes to thank Bishop Jimmie Williams for his belief in and generous support of this important book. Assembling a complex project with such historical significance requires faith, vision, and strength of purpose. Bishop Williams has an abundance of this, which allowed the book to become a reality. For this he is greatly admired and respected.

The publisher wishes to thank Ted Vernon for his kind assistance in getting this book across the finish line. His participation will forever be appreciated.

FROM THE AUTHOR

This book would be devoid of certain key elements were it not for diligent work of the remarkable professional investigator, Dan Reimer and his company, SOUTHFLORIDA PI. Researching this event from a by-gone era had many complexities and Mr. Reimer's remarkable expertise helped us to locate important participants who provided critical information about the life and times of Harry T. Moore.

Excellent writers, journalists, academics, historians, and authors have done fine work to document Harry T. Moore's life. A bibliography is provided at the conclusion of this volume to offer information about their exceptional books. Five authors deserve particular mention and gratitude. I have great respect for Ben Green, Gary Corsair, Gilbert King, Irvin D. S. Winsboro and Joseph North. Their many years of hard work and intense due diligence have produced impressive literary works with outstanding results.

Reverend Dr. O'Neal Dozier of the Worldwide Christian Center has been a supporter of this book from the beginning. His steadfast loyalty and active support have been invaluable while his kindness has been an inspiration.

As we go to print with this book, I felt it was important to acknowledge an important recent development in the Groveland Four case. On January 11th, 2019, Florida's Governor, Ron DeSantis and the Florida Executive Clemency Board granted pardons, posthumously, to the four young black men (the Groveland Four) who had been unjustly accused of rape in the criminal case that is seen as one of the most shameful symbols of Jim Crow racial injustice in America. It took America seventy years.

BIBLIOGRAPHY

Newton, Michael. *The Invisible Empire, The Ku Klux Klan in Florida.* Florida: University Press of Florida, 2001

Tushnet, Mark V. *The Library of Black America - Thurgood Marshall, His Speeches; Writing, Arguments, Opinions, and Reminiscences.* Chicago, Illinois: Lawrence Hill Books, an imprint of Chicago Review Press, Inc. Mark V. Tushnet, 2001

Green, Ben. *Before His Time, The Untold Story of Harry T. Moore, America's First Civil Rights Martyr.* New York: The Free Press, A Division of Simon & Schuster Inc., 1999

King, Gilbert. *Devil in the Grove, Thurgood Marshall, the Groveland Boys, and the Dawn of a New America.* New York: Harper Collins, 2012

Corsair, Gary. *Legal Lynching, The Sad Saga of the Groveland Four.* Florida: Gary Corsair, 2012

Radelet, Michael L./Bedau, Hugo Adam/Putnam, Constance E. *In Spite Of Innocence, Erroneous Convictions in Capital Cases.* Boston, Massachusetts: Northeastern University Press, 1992

North, Joseph. *Behind The Florida Bombings.* New York: New Century Publishers, 1952

Ebony Magazine. *The Bomb Heard Around The World.* Chicago, Illinois: Johnson Publishing Co. Inc., April 1952

Saunders, Sr. Robert W. *Bridging The Gap, Continuing the Florida NAACP Legacy of Harry T. Moore 1952-1966.* Florida: University of Tampa Press, 2000

Winsboro, Irvin D.S. *Florida's Freedom Struggle, The Black Experience from Colonial Time to the New Millennium.* Florida: The Florida Historical Society Press, 2010

Winsboro, Irvin D.S. *Old South, New South, or Down South? Florida and the Modern Civil Rights Movement.* West Virginia: West Virginia University Press, 2009

Rabby, Glenda Alice. *The Pain and the Promise, The Struggle for Civil Rights in Tallahassee.* Georgia: University of Georgia Press, 1999

Patterson, James T. *Brown v. Board of Education: A Civil Rights Milestone and Its Troubled Legacy.* New York: Oxford University Press, 2001

Weiner, Melissa F. *Power, Protest, and the Public Schools: Jewish and African American Struggles in New York City.* New York: Rutgers University Press, 2010

Thomas, Brook. *Plessy v. Ferguson: A Brief History with Documents.* Bedford Books, St. Martin's, First Edition (July 15, 1996)

Lofgren, Charles A. *The Plessy Case: A Legal-Historical Interpretation.* New York: Oxford University Press, 1987

Brands, H.W. *American Colossus.* New York: Anchor Books, A Division of Random House, Inc. 2010

Elliott, Mark. *Color-Blind Justice: Albion Tourgée and the Quest for Racial Equality from the Civil War to Plessy v. Ferguson.* New York: Oxford University Press, 2006

END NOTES

PAGES

16-17   *"Mims was a small town (and still is) located at the north end of Brevard County"*: Florida-Backroads-Travel.com, Mims, Florida, Mike Miller; June 1, 2018

17   *"Sat a tiny 'shotgun' house which was the home of Harry T. Moore."*: Juanita Barton Interview, April 5th, 2018

17-25   *"On Christmas Day in 1951"*: Florida Department of Law Enforcement (FDLE), Florida Attorney General Charlie Crist / Division of Civil Rights, Case # LO- 4 - 1358, December 21, 2004

17-25   *"On Christmas Day evening a sedan pulled over"*: Ben Green, Before His Time, The Untold Story of Harry T. Moore, America's First Civil Rights Martyr, New York: 1999 p. 3-11

22   *"Wife of Victim of Christmas Bombing Dies"*, News Headline, New York United Press/Herald Tribune, January 4, 1952

23-25   *"The St. James Missionary Baptist Church"*: Joseph North, Behind The Florida Bombings, New York: 1952 p. 7-10

17-25   *"On Christmas Day in 1951"*: Federal Bureau of Investigation (FBI), Case #44-4036, December 1951- September 1954

24   *"Bombing climaxed series of outrages"*: Ebony Magazine, "The Bomb Heard Around The World", April 1952

25-26   *"I came across the Groveland story"*: Author Gary Carsair Interview: April 6, 2018

26-27   *"Three weeks later the NAACP announced"*: Ben Green, Before His Time, The Untold Story of Harry T. Moore, America's First Civil Rights Martyr, New York: 1999 p. 194

27   *"No one's life can be encompassed in one telling"*: Ghandi (motion picture) John Richard Briley, 1982

28   *"Hate Bomb Kills NAACP Secretary"*, The African American Newspaper (AFRO) New York: January 5, 1952 (front page)

29   *"Harry T. Moore was a bold and courageous man"*: Florida Department of Law Enforcement (FDLE), Florida Attorney General Charlie Crist / Division of Civil Rights, Case # LO- 4 - 1358, December 21, 2004

30-31   *"Why are Harry and Harriette Moore"*: Engineer/Activist William Gary Interview, April 4, 2018

32-33   *"A Special Appeal to the religious, fraternal and civic leaders of Florida"*: NAACP letter written by Harry Moore with permission from Draper "Skip" Pagan (Evangeline Moore's son): October 14, 1947

34   *"Early on, Harry became the Executive Secretary"*: Florida Department of Law Enforcement (FDLE), Florida Attorney General Charlie Crist / Division of Civil Rights, Case # LO- 4 - 1358, December 21, 2004

34-35   *"When you were a teenager"*: Mims resident, Elouise Boatwrite Interview: April 2, 2018

END NOTES

PAGES

59-60　　"...*the Supreme Court's Plessy vs. Ferguson*": Plessy v. Ferguson, 163 U.S. 537(1896). Public domain material from U.S government document

60-62　　"*Meanwhile Lake County citrus company owners*": Federal Bureau of Investigation (FBI) Case File #44-4036, September 1954

60-62　　"*Meanwhile Lake County citrus company owners*": Florida Department of Law Enforcement (FDLE), Attorney General Charlie Crist/Division of Civil Rights, Case File # LO-4-1358, December 21, 2004

63　　　　"*The hooded hoodlums and sheeted jerks*": "Klan Fought in Florida, Governor Warren Assails Marchers, Says He Will Ask Legal Ban", New York Times. 29 January 1949. p. 7

64-67　　"*Bombing Climaxed Series of Outrages*": Ebony Magazine Article, "The Bomb Heard Around The World" reprinted, April 1952

66-67　　"*Speaking to the United Nations*": Joseph North, Behind The Florida Bombings, New York, 1952 p. 13-14

69　　　　"*My name is Walter Irvin.*": Court Transcript., Defendant's Letter to the court, 1949

70-73　　"*The three young men*": Gilbert King, Devil in the Grove, Thurgood Marshall, the Groveland Boys, and the Dawn of a New America, New York: 2012 p. 377-379

73-74　　"*Harry Moore stood up to Sheriff McCall*": Gary Carsair, Author, Interview Cont'd: April 2, 2018

75-80　　"*Commencing in 1951 there had been over a dozen*": Alison Bethel Interview, former Director Civil Rights, Attorney General Charlie Crist, Interview: April 12, 2018

75-80　　"*Many incendiary events occurred in Florida*": Dennis Norred, former Special Agent Interview, Federal Florida Department of Law Enforcement, Florida, Attorney General Charlie Crist, FDLE Case File # LO-4-1358, April 3, 2018

75-80　　"*There were banner headlines*": Gilbert King, Devil in the Grove, Thurgood Marshall, the Groveland Boys, and the Dawn of a New America, New York: 2012 p. 445-446

86-88　　"*Harry knew he was crossing over the line*": Dennis Norred, former Special Agent Interview, Ibid, April 3, 2018

86-90　　"*Harry knew he was crossing the line*": Florida Department of Law Enforcement (FDLE), Civil Rights Office, Case File # LO-4-1358, December 21, 2004

90-91　　"*But American anger sprung up*": Gilbert King, Devil in the Grove, Ibid. p. 445-447

90-91　　"*William L. Patterson, Head of the Civil Rights Congress*": Joseph North, Behind The Florida Bombings, Ibid p.4

91　　　　"*A tragic irony of all this is that lynching*": The New York Times, "3 Black U.S. Senators Introduce Bill to Make Lynching a Federal hate Crime", New York, June 29, 2018

92　　　　"*Charles W. Cherry Sr. believed in equal rights*": Florida Press Association, July 2018

93　　　　"*In my own opinion*": Interview quote, Florida Department of Law Enforcement (FDLE), Attorney General Charlie Crist/Division of Civil Rights, Case File # LO-4-1358, December

PAGES

96   *"He was first appointed"*: Anthony Summers "The secret life of J Edgar Hoover", The
          Guardian, January 1, 2012 p.74-105

96-97   *"Some say he was a controversial figure"*: John Stuart Cox, Athan G. Theoharis, The Boss: J.
          Edgar Hoover and the Great American Inquisition. Temple University Press, 1988 p. 108

97-101   *"In an article published"*: Betty Medsger, The Nation, "Just Being Black Was Enough to Get
          Yourself Spied on by J. Edgar Hoover's FBI", https://www.thenation.com/article/just-
          being-black-was-enough-get-yourself-spied-j-edgar-hoovers-fbi/ January 22, 2014,
          originating from the book "The Burglary: The Discovery of J. Edgar Hoover's Secret FBI",
          A Borzoi Book, Published by Alfred A. Knopf, a division of Random House, LLC, New
          York, 2014

101   *"We want no Gestapo or secret police"*: Quote from President Harry S. Truman, Truman Papers,
          President's Secretary's Files, May 12, 1945

105-107   *"The Red Scare had taken hold"* Murray B. Levin, Political Hysteria in America: The
          Democratic Capacity for Repression, Basic Books, 1971 p. 29

106-110   *"McCarthy became the poster boy"*: Arthur *Herman," Joseph McCarthy: Reexamining the Life and
          Legacy of America's Most Hated Senator", Free Press, 1999 p. 264.*

110   *"Senator McCarthy - Opportunity Keeps Knocking"*: Time Magazine Cover, March 28, 1954

111   *"We were at war"*: Edna Chappelle McKenzie, Journalist, Pittsburgh Courier, 1943

111-117   *"America's entering World War II created an opportunity"*: Maria Hohn, African-American
          GI's World War II: Fight for democracy abroad and at home, Vassar College/The
          Conversation/AP, January 30, 2018

115-117   *"Edna Chappelle McKenzie was an award-winning journalist"*: The Black Press: Soldiers Without
          Swords, The California Newsreel, July 2, 2018

124-127   *"Before the deaths of the Moores"*: Florida Goes to War: The Sunshine State in WWII,   Florida
          Humanities Council (FHC) , state affiliate of the National Endowment for the
          Humanities, June 18, 2018

127-129   *"The Origin of the name Jump Jim Crow"*: Wikipedia, The Free Encyclopedia, Wikimedia
          Foundation, June 27, 2017

131 -132 "Stetson was a highly-regarded author": The Stetson Family Trust, Stetson Kennedy
          Foundation, Florida, May 18, 2018

130-131   *"Not long after Hitler rose to power"*: Albert Einstein, Civil Rights Activist, Snopes.com
          July 2, 2018

133-134   *"Because Einstein was a foreigner"*: Dennis Overbye, New York Times, "New Details Emerge
          From the Einstein Files; How the F.B.I. Tracked His Phone Calls and His Trash",
          May 7, 2002

138-140   *"Michael E. Ruane comments"*: Michael E. Ruane, "You are done: A secret letter to Martin
          Luther King Jr. sheds light on FBI's malice", Retropolis, The Washington Post,
          December 13, 2017

139   "J. Edgar Hoover letter": James. L Swanson letter, which appears in Retropolis website, The
          Washington Post and in his books "Chasing King's Killer, "The Hunt for Martin Luther
          King Jr.'s Assassin", Scholastic Press, New York

END NOTES

PAGES

142   "The Grand Jury reconvened on February 5": Ben Green, Before His Time, The Untold
         Story of Harry T. Moore, America's First Civil Rights Martyr, New York: 1999 p. 195

141-144 "Hoover's track record, where race was concerned": Ben Green, Before His Time, The
         Untold Story of Harry T. Moore, America's First Civil Rights Martyr, New York: 1999
         p. 193-197

142-145 "*By summer of 1952*": Joseph North, Behind The Florida Bombings, New York,
         1952 p. 12-14

143   "*Achtung! Nieder Mit die Verdammte*": Behind The Florida Bombings, Ibid p. 14

144   "*Can you imagine what India feels*": Behind The Florida Bombings, Ibid p. 13-14

146   "*Transcription of a letter Governor Warren*": Progressive Voters' League letter written by Harry
         Moore with permission from Draper "Skip" Pagan (Evangeline Moore's son) no date

152-153 "*In June, the grand jury handed down seven indictments*": Ben Green, Before His Time, Ibid
         p.196-197

154   "*Separate but Equal is a phrase most of us*": Wikipedia, Wikimedia Foundation

154   "*In 1954, all of America had shifted*": Apartheid was established in South Africa":
         Encyclopaedia Brittanica, June 10, 2018

156   "Brown v. Board of Education, 347 U.S. 483, This article incorporates public domain
         material from this U.S government document,1954

157   "*A seamstress from a department store*": National Archives, "An Act of Courage, The Arrest
         Records of Rosa Parks", U.S. National Archives and Records Administration, June 12, 2018

158-159 "*After the Supreme Court's desegregation decision*": Ben Green, Before His Time, Ibid
         p. 96-197

160-161 "*Unbeknownst to most Americans*": Irvin D.S. Winsboro, Florida's Freedom Struggle,
         The Black Experience from Colonial Time to the New Millennium, Florida, 2010
         p. 4-11, 153-158

163-169 "*The FBI investigation began*": Federal Bureau of Investigation, Case File: # 44-4036
         December 1951-September 1954

170-172 "*It was Brevard County Sheriff Roland Zimmerman*": Brevard County Sheriff's Office
         Investigation, 1978

172-176 "*In 1991, the Governor of Florida, Lawton Chiles*": FDLE Investigation
         Case #E1-91-26-016, 1991

176-219 "*Charlie Crist is an American attorney*": Attorney General Charlie Crist / FDLE/Civil Rights
         Office, Case #44-4036 & Case number #PE-01-0048, 2004

221-222 "*Only three and a half years after*": News Headlines, Writers John Bacon, Jerry Mitchell,
         "Feds Open Emmett Till Murder Case", USA TODAY July 12, 2018

222-225 "*First Corinthians Chapter 13*": Speech by Evangeline Moore for her father, with
         permission from Draper "Skip" Pagan (Evangeline Moore's son): December 2003

226-229 "*I knew them from childhood*": Friend of the Moore Family Lucy Seigler Interview,
         April 2, 2018

232   "*In 2008, the FBI initiated a review*": Federal Bureau of Investigation/Cold Case Initiative
         The Final Investigation, March 20, 2017 Case closed.